Water Cycles

The source of life
from start to finish

DK Penguin Random House

Authors and consultants:
Lead consultant Derek Harvey
Plants and Animals authors Steve Setford,
Anita Ganeri, and Lizzie Munsey
Prehistory author and consultant Emily Keeble
Biology author Emily Dodd
Space author and consultant Sophie Allan
Technology and humans author and consultant Clive Gifford
Earth consultant Anthea Lacchia
Earth and Weather authors Anita Ganeri,
Steve Setford, John Farndon, and Lizzie Munsey
Weather consultant John Farndon

Illustrated by Sam Falconer

Senior editor Carrie Love
Designer Charlotte Milner

US Editor Jane Perlmutter
US Senior editor Shannon Beatty
Additional editing Marie Greenwood, Jolyon Goddard
Additional designing Rachael Hare, Robert Perry, Karen Hood,
and Claire Patane
DTP designer Sachin Gupta
Picture researchers Rituraj Singh and Vagisha Pushp
Managing editor Penny Smith
Managing art editor Mabel Chan
Pre-producer Robert Dunn
Producer John Casey
Publishing director Sarah Larter

First American Edition, 2021
Published in the United States by DK Publishing
1745 Broadway, 20th Floor, New York, NY 10019

Copyright © 2021 Dorling Kindersley Limited
DK, a Division of Penguin Random House LLC
24 25 10 9 8 7 6 5 4
010–321055–July/2021

Published in Great Britain by Dorling Kindersley Limited.

A catalog record for this book is available from
the Library of Congress.
ISBN: 978-0-7440-3334-2
DK books are available at special discounts when purchased in
bulk for sales promotions, premiums, fund-raising, or educational
use. For details, contact: DK Publishing Special Markets, 1745
Broadway, 20th Floor, New York, NY 10019
SpecialSales@dk.com

Printed and bound in China

All images © Dorling Kindersley Limited
For further information see: www.dkimages.com

For the curious
www.dk.com

MIX
Paper from
responsible sources
FSC™ C018179
www.fsc.org

This book was made with Forest
Stewardship Council™ certified
paper – one small step in DK's
commitment to a sustainable future.
For more information go to
www.dk.com/our-green-pledge

Water
Cycles

The source of life
from start to finish

Contents

Life in water

Water and humans

What is *water?*

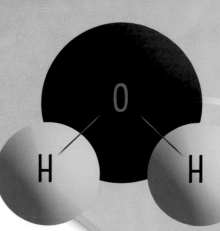

Scientists give water the special code name of H_2O, to show how its molecules are made up.

With no color, taste, or smell, water may seem a little boring. But, it is actually an amazing natural substance that makes our planet special. Without water, there would be no life on Earth.

Most water on Earth is liquid. However, at 212° F (100° C) it becomes an invisible gas called water vapor, and below 32° F (0° C) it turns to solid ice. The smallest pieces of water are called molecules. Attracting (pulling) forces between water molecules make the molecules "stick" together to form puddles, lakes, and oceans, while still allowing the water to flow easily.

Water molecules are also attracted to many other materials. This makes water great at dissolving things—it pulls them apart so that they mix with the water. Wherever water flows, through soil or through plants and animals, it carries dissolved minerals, nutrients, and other chemicals that are vital for life.

In addition to making life on Earth possible, water molds the land and coasts through falling rain, rushing rivers, slow-moving glaciers, and crashing ocean waves.

Life giving and planet shaping—water is truly amazing.

If this pond froze solid, the animals and plants in it would die.

Floating ice

Ice floats on water because it is lighter. This is important for aquatic life. When ice forms on the surface, it shields the water below from the cold air above, stopping the rest of the water—and the things that live in it—from freezing too.

Water molecules

Water molecules are made up of tiny pieces of matter called atoms. Each water molecule has two hydrogen atoms that join a single oxygen atom by forces called bonds.

Some small, light creatures can walk over ponds without breaking the water's "skin."

Surface skin

When molecules at the surface of water pull on each other, they make the water behave as though it has a thin "skin." This is called surface tension.

Surface tension pulls water into round droplets.

An unbroken stream of water travels up very thin tubes inside plants.

Shaping the land

Water can break up rocks into particles and carry them away. The Grand Canyon in Arizona, US, was carved out by the waters of the Colorado River over millions of years.

The Grand Canyon is 6,000 ft (1,800 m) deep and 18 miles (29 km) wide.

Sticky water

The "stickiness" of water molecules is why water makes things wet. This "stickiness" also keeps the stream of water rising up inside the stem of a plant. The water rises in continuous, unbroken columns, from the roots to the leaves—even when that plant is a towering tree.

Some materials, such as oil, repel water. An oily coating on the feathers of waterbirds, such as this gannet, keeps the feathers dry.

Earth's water

Nearly all the water on Earth is salty. The small amount of freshwater that's on Earth is mostly frozen ice or lies hidden underground. There is only a very small amount of fresh, liquid water on the planet's surface.

Atmospheric water

There is water in the air. It takes the form of invisible water vapor and tiny droplets of liquid water that clump together as clouds.

Groundwater

Almost a third of Earth's freshwater seeps below the planet's surface. This is called groundwater, and it is mostly held within tiny cracks in rocks.

Saltwater

While most saltwater is in seas and oceans, there are saltwater lakes on Earth's surface. There are also reserves of saltwater underground.

Freshwater

Rivers, lakes, swamps, and marshes are vital sources of water for many living things. The freshwater we use largely comes from rivers and lakes.

Ice

About two-thirds of all Earth's freshwater is frozen on the surface as glaciers, ice sheets, or snow. Some of it is permafrost—water frozen in the ground.

Soil

There is about the same amount of water in the soil as there is in the air, held between soil particles. Plants need soil water to survive.

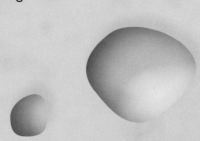

Water in living things

Living things are made mostly of water. But the proportion of water in the body varies between different organisms. While water makes up just over half of the human body, jellyfish are almost entirely water.

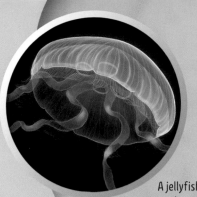

A jellyfish is about 95 percent water, but water makes up only 50–60 percent of an adult human.

Water in space

Earth is the only planet in the solar system with bodies of liquid water on its surface. There is, however, ice on Mars and on the moons of some planets. There are also lumps of ice and dust, called comets, that hurtle around the solar system. Scientists are discovering new planets, far away in other galaxies, that may have water.

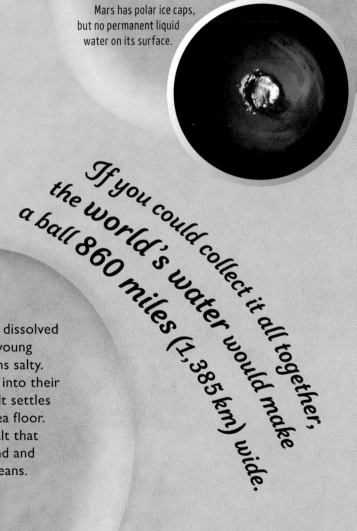

Mars has polar ice caps, but no permanent liquid water on its surface.

Where is *water*?

Seen from space, Earth is a mostly blue planet. The blue is the water of seas, oceans, lakes, and rivers. Water covers about three-quarters of our world. But not all of Earth's water lies on the surface. There is also water in the air, in the ground, and in living things—including ourselves.

If you could collect it all together, the world's water would make a ball 860 miles (1,385 km) wide.

Why is the sea salty?

Billions of years ago, water dissolved salt from the rocks of the young Earth and turned the oceans salty. Marine organisms take salt into their bodies, and some ocean salt settles and becomes part of the sea floor. This is replaced by more salt that dissolves from rocks on land and is then washed into the oceans.

Rivers carry dissolved salt into seas and oceans, keeping up their salt levels.

When water evaporates from the ocean into the air, the salt is left behind—which is why rain falls as freshwater.

Cycles and water

A cycle is a repeating series of events, such as the rising and setting of the sun or the changing of the seasons. Water is involved in many cycles. Earth's water is always on the move—passing through many parts of the planet in different ways, and in different forms.

Our daily water

The water we use in our daily lives comes from the water cycle (see right). It is taken out of rivers and lakes or from deep underground. Then it is cleaned and pumped to our homes. After we have used it, the water is put back into rivers or the sea.

To avoid harming wildlife, dirty wastewater from our homes is cleaned before it is returned to the water cycle.

Moving through life

Water is involved in the chemical processes inside living things that keep them alive. Organisms take in water from their surroundings, it passes through them, and they expel it with their waste.

Animals must drink often to replace the water they lose when they breathe, poop, and pee.

*The amount of water on Earth **never changes**—the water just gets used again and again.*

2 Water at the ocean's surface evaporates—it changes into water vapor that rises into the air.

1 The sun's heat warms the ocean.

The life cycle of the European eel is spent partly in saltwater and partly in freshwater.

Amphibians have life cycles that switch between water and land.

Life cycles in water

Watery habitats, such as rivers, marshes, rocky shores, coral reefs, and the open ocean, provide places where organisms can live and thrive. The pattern of being born, growing, producing young, and dying is called a life cycle.

Water vapor

In water vapor, the molecules can move freely, so the gas spreads out.

Liquid water

Molecules in liquid water move more than those in ice, allowing water to flow.

Ice

Water molecules in ice are held tightly together and cannot move, giving ice a fixed shape.

The water cycle

The world's water is constantly circulating between the ocean, atmosphere, and land. Called the water cycle, this nonstop process is powered by the sun's energy. As the water circulates, it frequently changes between liquid, solid, and gas as it gains and loses heat.

5 Water droplets in clouds may freeze into ice crystals called snowflakes.

6 Snow builds up to form ice rivers called glaciers.

3 Water vapor cools and condenses into tiny water droplets that form clouds. The water droplets build up in clouds until they eventually fall as rain.

4 Plants absorb water with their roots and release water vapor from their leaves.

7 Glacier ice melts back to water.

8 Rivers carry water from rain and melted snow and ice back into the ocean.

9 Some water makes its way to the ocean by traveling through rocks underground.

11

Water on Earth

Water constantly ebbs and flows on our amazing planet. It falls from the sky, rushes down mountains, and flows through seas and oceans—forever circulating through the global water cycle. Water brings us different types of weather and a variety of habitats. It alters coastlines, carves out caves, and changes landscapes.

The *power* of *water*

Water is everywhere in nature. It has the strength to carve out landscapes and change coastlines. It forms gently flowing streams and fast-moving, cascading waterfalls. Water helps determine whether a place will be dry and empty or green, luscious, and full of life.

Hurricanes bring heavy rain and strong winds.

Some mountains and trees are blanketed in snow all year. In other places, they are only covered in certain months.

Types of weather

Weather is the state of the atmosphere at a particular place and time. Water plays an important role in weather conditions. Wet weather is due to precipitation—drizzle, rain, sleet, snow, or hail. If it's hot and humid outside it's because there is more water in the atmosphere. Different types of weather affect the climate of particular areas on Earth.

Large hailstones fall from the sky with such force that they can damage buildings.

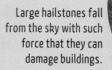

Rainbows are formed when light shines through water droplets that are still in the sky after it's stopped raining.

Flooding after heavy rainfall can cause chaos. Sadly, because of climate change, flooding is happening more and more.

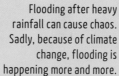

Altering coastlines

Low-lying land and coastlines are threatened when sea levels rise. They are rising right now because of climate change. A warmer climate melts ice in glaciers and ice sheets on land. The warmth also makes the ocean water expand. More than 600 million people live in coastal areas less than 33 ft (10 m) above sea level. These coastlines must be protected now.

Huge icebergs, such as this one in Antarctica, are home to ice-dwelling animals.

The Sand Engine in the Netherlands is a man-made sand deposit along the coast, built to protect the low-lying land from seawater.

Water and life

All life depends on water. Most animals and plants contain a lot of water. Forests thrive where there is plenty of rain to help them grow. Billions of creatures actually live in the water—in oceans, rivers, and lakes. And many, such as frogs, spend much of their lives in the water as well as on land. Some microbes can actually live inside the ice of polar regions.

Lush vegetation relies on frequent rainfall and moist conditions.

Niagara Falls is on the border of Canada and the US. About 70 Olympic-size swimming pools of water go over the falls every minute.

Changing landscapes

Water has the power to shape nature. It can happen quickly, such as when heavy rainfall causes flooding, or it can occur slowly, such as when land is eroded. It takes many years for water to erode rocks and, for example, to form caves. Waterfalls also form over time—created by the powerful force of river water wearing down soft rocks.

Water helps create unusual rock formations, such as stalactites, found in caves—as in this cave in New Mexico.

Making *and* losing oceans

Throughout Earth's history, the oceans have changed dramatically. As the continents moved, oceans widened and shrank. Changes in sea level caused continents to flood or provided bridges between landmasses. The changing oceans have shaped the evolution of life on Earth.

Snowball earth

The most dramatic ice age in Earth's history may have locked most or all of the oceans in ice or slush, dramatically lowering sea level. Scientists call this the Snowball Earth hypothesis.

Some scientists think that part of Earth's water may have come from asteroids.

Oxygenation

Layers of rusted iron, called banded-iron formations, show when Earth started to become rich in oxygen. The oxygen was produced by early forms of life through photosynthesis.

Earth's formation

First oceans

The young Earth was once too hot for liquid water to exist for long on the surface. Once Earth had cooled, ocean basins began to fill with water that had been locked up in the rocks that formed the planet. These oceans allowed life to begin.

Today, about 1.7 percent of Earth's water is in ice caps and glaciers.

4.54 bya

4.4 bya

3.5 bya

700 mya

bya = billion years ago
mya = million years ago

16

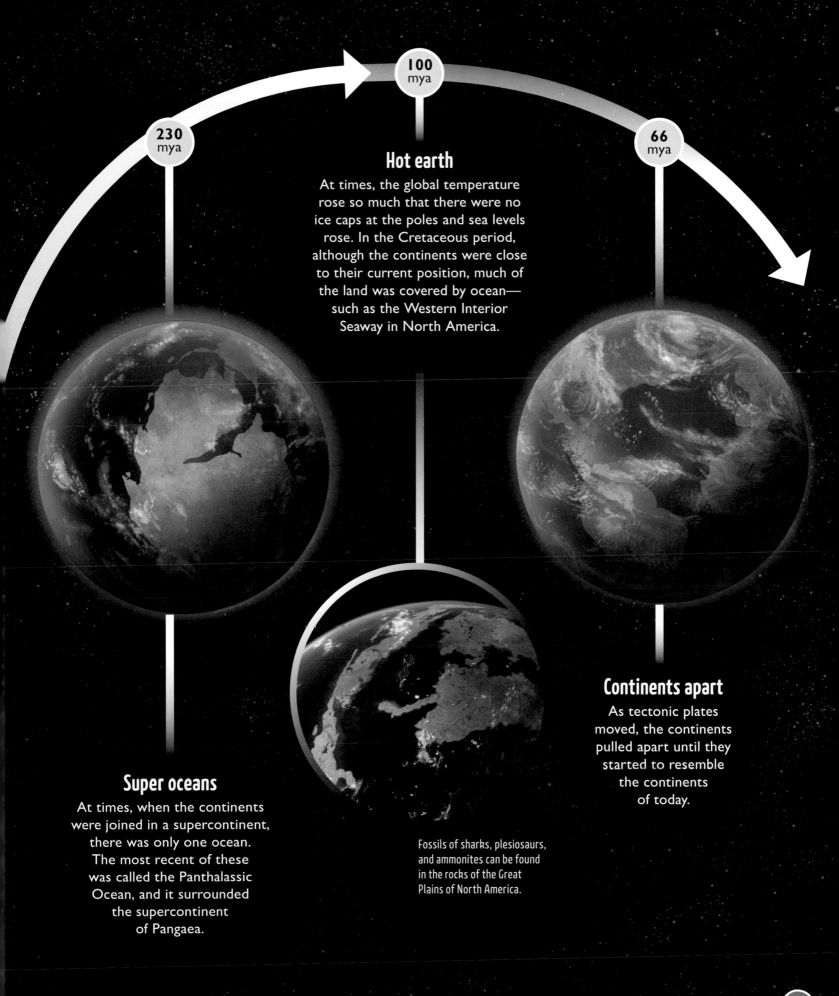

Hot earth

At times, the global temperature rose so much that there were no ice caps at the poles and sea levels rose. In the Cretaceous period, although the continents were close to their current position, much of the land was covered by ocean— such as the Western Interior Seaway in North America.

Continents apart

As tectonic plates moved, the continents pulled apart until they started to resemble the continents of today.

Super oceans

At times, when the continents were joined in a supercontinent, there was only one ocean. The most recent of these was called the Panthalassic Ocean, and it surrounded the supercontinent of Pangaea.

Fossils of sharks, plesiosaurs, and ammonites can be found in the rocks of the Great Plains of North America.

Clouds

All clouds—from wispy, white clouds high in the sky to dark-gray rain clouds—are made from tiny water droplets or ice crystals. You can see clouds because the droplets or crystals reflect light from the sun. Follow the life cycle of a dramatic thundercloud, or cumulonimbus.

Forming a cloud

A cloud develops when millions upon millions of water droplets or ice crystals form together. As more warm air rises and more water condenses, the cloud grows taller and wider. This kind of heaped cloud is called a cumulus cloud.

Cooling down

As the water vapor rises, it expands and cools down and condenses onto dust and other tiny particles in the air. This turns the vapor into tiny droplets or frozen ice crystals.

Water droplets

Warming up

The sun warms water in the ocean or in lakes, or the soil and plants. It then evaporates and turns into water vapor. The warm, moist air floats upward into cooler air.

More water evaporates when the ocean or land is heated by warm sunshine.

Lightning
Strong air currents in a thundercloud can smash droplets and crystals together, creating static electricity. The electricity can jump though the cloud or between the cloud and ground as a lightning flash.

Floating fog
We think of clouds as being high up in the sky, but a cloud can form at ground level, too. When this happens, it is called fog. This picture shows fog forming in a mountainous valley.

Mature cloud

When a huge amount of warm air rises at the same time, a cumulus cloud grows larger. It becomes supertall and is called a cumulonimbus cloud. Inside the giant cloud, water droplets and ice crystals move up and down on strong air currents. Rain falls from the cloud when water droplets grow large enough to fall to the ground.

Raindrops

Water droplets

The water droplets come together to make raindrops.

Inside the cloud some ice crystals melt to become tiny water droplets.

Large raindrops

Ice crystals

The drops grow until they are heavy enough to fall from the cloud.

Large raindrops often break up into smaller drops as they fall.

Falling raindrops

End of a cloud

Eventually, warm air stops rising into the cloud, or the cloud mixes with dry, warm air around it. At this stage, no more water vapor can condense. The cloud shrinks and dies away.

See also
Find out about the different types of clouds (20–21) and how they form.

Rain falls to the ground.

Clouds in space There are clouds surrounding other planets too! Unlike Earth's clouds, however, they are not made up of water droplets. The clouds around other planets, such as the cold, swirly clouds that surround Jupiter, are made of gases and dust.

Water that falls to Earth from the sky is **called precipitation.** *It can be liquid water—* **rain—or frozen, as sleet or snow.**

Cloud types

There are three main types of clouds. Their Latin names describe their shape—cirrus (wispy), cumulus (heaped), and stratus (sheet). By adding words to these names, we can describe other types of clouds. For example, stratocumulus means "heaped sheets of cloud." Some clouds can form very high up in the sky, while others are much closer to the ground.

Cirrus Thin, wispy-looking cirrus clouds are made of ice crystals. They form very high up in the air.

Cirrocumulus These small, fluffy clouds sometimes form when cirrostratus clouds break up.

Cirrostratus These thin, flat clouds make the sky look gray and overcast. They are a sign that it might rain in a day or two.

High-level

Cumulonimbus These huge, tall clouds spread from low-level to high-level. They can cause thunderstorms with heavy rain, hail, and lightning.

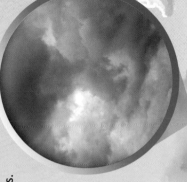

Altocumulus Small, puffy, white clouds like this are sometimes called cloudlets.

Stratocumulus These low, puffy, gray clouds may produce a little rain, and can turn into nimbostratus clouds.

Nimbostratus Thick, dark, and gray, nimbostratus clouds usually bring hours of rain or snow.

Altostratus These thin sheets of clouds turn the sky dark gray—usually a sign that rain is coming.

Stratus Sheets of stratus clouds often cover a lot of the sky. They can be white or gray, and may produce light rain or drizzle.

Cumulus Fluffy, white cumulus clouds often form in warm weather, when warm air rises up into the cooler sky. They can turn into cumulonimbus.

Mid-level

Low-level

Hurricanes

These fierce swirling storms cover huge distances, bringing superstrong winds, heavy rain, and flooding along coasts. The life cycle of a hurricane typically lasts about nine days. Depending on which part of the world they occur in, these spectacular storms are known as hurricanes, cyclones, or typhoons.

Thunderstorms form when warm, damp air rises into the atmosphere and then cools down to form clouds.

Thunderstorms

Hurricanes begin with a group of thunderstorms. The storms often grow over warm tropical waters to the north and south of the equator. This first stage of a hurricane is called a tropical disturbance.

Decay

When a hurricane moves over cooler water or over land, it begins to lose energy. The winds slow down. Eventually, it weakens into a tropical storm, and finally dies away completely.

Hitting land

Hurricanes start out in the ocean. They move across the water and sometimes hit land. Beneath the hurricane, sea level can rise by up to 20 ft (6 m). This sudden rise is called a storm surge and—along with huge waves created by the hurricane's winds—causes flooding along the coast. Strong wind and heavy rain also damage buildings.

Buildings are flooded by seawater and battered by winds.

Spinning

More air rushes in to replace the moist air rising up. This pulls air into the base of the storm, making winds blow. Because the Earth is rotating on its axis, these winds begin to swirl, and the storm begins to spin.

Storms spin counterclockwise in the Northern Hemisphere and clockwise in the Southern Hemisphere.

The cloudless center of the hurricane is called the eye, and the strongest winds surround it.

74 mph

Warm air keeps rising into the cloud bands.

Cooler air descends back downward in the spaces between the bands of cloud.

See also
Find out more about cloud types (20–21) and how a cloud (18–19) forms.

Full-blown hurricane

As it moves over the warm water below, the storm picks up energy. When its winds rise above 39 mph (63 kph), the storm officially becomes a tropical storm. It keeps growing, and its winds get stronger. When the winds reach 74 mph (119 kph), the storm is now officially called a hurricane.

Hurricane scales
The strength of a hurricane is shown on a scale. Different scales are used in different parts of the world. The Saffir-Simpson scale, for example, is used in the Atlantic Ocean and some parts of the Pacific.

Hurricane giant
This 1979 hurricane is the largest and most powerful hurricane ever witnessed. It was 1,380 miles (2,220 km) wide.

Hurricane hunters
Research airplanes fly into hurricanes to collect data on air pressure and wind speeds. It's a very bumpy ride!

Snowflake

Snow falls from clouds, just like rain, sleet, and hail. It is made up of tiny crystals called snowflakes that land on the ground as fluffy, white snow. Every snowflake contains about 50 ice crystals. No two snowflakes are the same!

A speck of dust

A snowflake begins its life as a tiny speck of dust inside a cloud. Water vapor sticks to the dust, forming a droplet of water.

Crystals grow

The corners of the crystal pick up more water vapor, forming little arms. All snowflakes have exactly six arms, because of the specific pattern that water molecules make when water freezes.

The snowflake falls

Although the number of arms is always the same, every snowflake grows into a unique shape. Its shape depends on the temperature of the air and how wet the cloud is. As it grows bigger and heavier, the snowflake begins to fall.

An ice ball forms

The droplet freezes, forming a ball of ice. As more water vapor in the cloud sticks to the ball, it grows into an ice crystal.

See also
Discover the three main types of clouds (20–21).

Melted snow evaporates

Eventually, the snowflake reaches the ground. When the snow melts, the water evaporates and the cycle starts again.

A snowflake begins to fall when it has grown enough to be heavier than the air around it.

Expecting snow? On high mountaintops and in polar regions, there is a permanent cover of snow or ice. Elsewhere, the heaviest snow falls when the air is just above freezing.

Snowy snuggles About 90 percent of snow that's settled on the ground is air. The air can't move and carry heat away with it, so snow is a good insulator. Many animals, such as polar bears, burrow in it to keep warm.

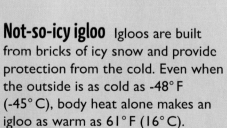

Not-so-icy igloo Igloos are built from bricks of icy snow and provide protection from the cold. Even when the outside is as cold as -48°F (-45°C), body heat alone makes an igloo as warm as 61°F (16°C).

A river's source

Clouds bring rain and snow to hills and mountains. Rain flows off the land into small channels, forming streams. In the spring, melting snow adds water to the streams. The streams flow down steep hillsides, tumbling across rocks and over waterfalls.

The Amazon River empties about 196,841 tons (200,000 tonnes) of water into the Atlantic Ocean every second.

A young river cuts a V-shaped valley into the landscape.

Cutting valleys

As the river flows downhill, it carves out valleys, gorges, and canyons. Smaller rivers that join the main river are called tributaries. The water and rocks that bump along the riverbed slowly wear it away. The water carries sediment (pebbles, sand, and silt) downstream. The process of rocks being worn into sediment is called weathering. Erosion happens when the sediment gets carried away.

S-bends

Bends form when one bank of the river is eroded more than the other. Gradually, the river gets more and more twisty. The bends are called meanders.

River

A river starts its life as a trickling stream in hills or mountains. On its journey to the ocean, it is joined by other streams and rivers and grows bigger. Rivers erode the landscape, wearing rocks away and gouging out valleys and canyons. Flowing rivers are part of the water cycle.

See also
Find out more about how water cycles work (10-11).

Water vapor made by evaporation forms clouds.

River's mouth
The river meets the ocean at its mouth, where it often splits into different channels. Sometimes, the river widens out to form an estuary, where the river water mixes with seawater. Some water evaporates from the ocean into the atmosphere, and will eventually fall as rain, and flow down a river again.

Flood plains
When the river floods over its banks it dumps sediment on the land on each side, creating flat areas called floodplains.

Oxbow lakes
During a flood, the river can break through the space between one bend and the next, cutting off the bend in between. The cutoff section is known as an oxbow lake.

Ephemeral rivers Some rivers, called ephemeral rivers, dry up for part of the year. They only flow for a few days after heavy rain.

Canyons The Grand Canyon in the US has been carved out by the Colorado River. The canyon is up to 18 miles (29 km) wide and up to 6,000 ft (1,800 m) deep.

Deltas A delta is an area of land at the end of a river, made up of sediment carried down the river. The sediment is dumped as the river slows when it flows into a sea or an ocean.

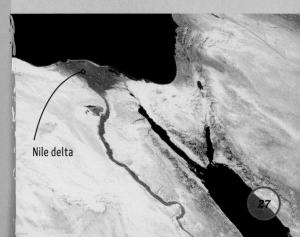

Nile delta

Waterfall

Cascading waterfalls are among Earth's most spectacular natural features. They are created when the powerful erosive force of river water wears away soft rocks, leaving a rocky ledge for the water to pour over.

Moving upstream

The overhanging ledge of hard rock is no longer supported, and collapses into the plunge pool. This cycle of erosion causes the position of the waterfall to slowly move upstream.

See also

Discover how a river (26–27) is made.

The river flows over the edge made by the hard rock.

Overhang

Chunks of rock break off and topple into the plunge pool below. The rocky debris swirls around in the bottom of the plunge pool, adding to the erosion of the softer rock behind the waterfall, creating an overhang of hard rock.

Hard and soft rock

Waterfalls start to form when a river flows over a layer of hard rock that has softer rock lying beneath. The water erodes the soft rock quicker than the hard rock, making the riverbed steeper on the soft rock.

Soft rocks such as shale and siltstone get worn away more easily than hard rocks such as granite.

The riverbed gets steeper as more soft rock is eroded.

Erosion

Over time, more soft rock is eroded by the force of the water and by stones that are pushed along by the flow, creating a step in the riverbed.

Plunge pool

The fast-flowing water erodes a hole in the rock called a plunge pool. Now, the water falls vertically into the hole and a young waterfall is formed.

More erosion cuts the soft rock away behind the waterfall.

The force of falling water makes the water swirl around in the pool.

You can sometimes see a rainbow in the mist around the falling water.

Water from the pool flows away down the river.

The highest falls are the Angel Falls, Venezuela at 3,212 ft (979 m)

Frozen falls In winter, a waterfall can freeze solid. The river stops flowing, and huge icicles dangle down. Ice climbers enjoy tackling frozen waterfalls.

Stepped falls Many waterfalls drop down in a series of steps. One of the most spectacular stepped falls is the Iguazu Falls on the border between Argentina and Brazil in South America.

Groundwater

Water hidden away inside rocks under the ground is called groundwater. It makes up nearly a third of the world's freshwater. Underground, water seeps into cracks and the tiny holes in porous rock. It flows slowly downhill through the rocks, in the same way that water soaks through sand. Some of the water emerges onto the surface again. This flow is part of the water cycle. Groundwater is an important source of water in many parts of the world.

Clouds and rain

When air rises and cools, the water vapor inside turns back into liquid water or ice, forming clouds. Rain and snow fall from the clouds onto the ground.

Evaporation

Water evaporates from the ground, the ocean, lakes, and plants. The water loss from plants is called transpiration. All of this adds water vapor to the atmosphere.

We can find water on land by digging a well down to below the water table.

Emerging from the ground

If the water table reaches the surface, water emerges from the ground in the form of springs, and streams flow from them. The water table alongside rivers and lakes is at the same level as the water surface.

Pollution Pesticides, fertilizers, and chemicals from waste buried in the ground often end up in groundwater, and pollute it. This can make it dangerous for people and animals who drink water from wells and streams.

Sinkholes Groundwater dissolves some rocks, such as limestone, creating underground spaces. If the roof of such a space collapses, a sinkhole appears in the ground. Sinkholes can damage buildings and roads.

Into the ground

Water that falls on the ground soaks into the soil. Some of it evaporates, some is used by plants, and some trickles down to the rock beneath the soil. The water can seep into permeable rocks—which are porous, with tiny holes—such as sandstone.

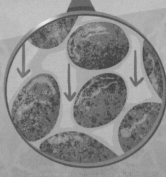

The water table

Lower down in the ground, the rock is completely saturated—the small spaces inside the rock are filled with water. The top of this saturated layer is called the water table. When there is a lot of rain, the water table rises. During a dry period, it falls. The mass of saturated rock below the water table is called an aquifer.

Above the water table, water coats the outside of the rock particles—but it does not fill the spaces in between.

Below the water table, water flows slowly through the spaces between the rock particles.

Underground flow

Groundwater flows very slowly downhill, through the rocks. It flows in permeable rocks, but cannot flow through impermeable rocks—such as granite and clay—which do not absorb water. Groundwater can stay underground for thousands of years.

See also Read about water in caves (34–35) and hot springs (32–33).

Oases An oasis is a place in a desert where groundwater comes to the surface, usually through cracks in the rock below. The water forms a pond from which plants and animals can get water.

Hot springs

Springs of warm water are a sure sign that something is happening beneath Earth's surface. They occur when hot molten rock, called magma, heats water deep underground and drives it up to the surface. In some hot springs, called geysers, water doesn't well up steadily—instead, high pressure fires jets of water and steam into the air.

Fumarole

The rising hot water may turn into steam before it reaches the surface. The steam, along with volcanic gases from the magma, billows out of openings known as fumaroles.

See also
Discover deep-sea vents (50–51)—jets of hot water found in the darkest depths of the ocean.

Hot spring

The heated water rises back up to the surface. It emerges through an opening, or vent, and forms a pool on the surface called a hot spring. The spring is fed by a constant supply of hot water from below.

Sulfur gases may give the steamy cloud an eggy smell.

Groundwater

Cold groundwater builds up as water from rain and snow works its way underground through layers of rock riddled with cracks.

Water heater

Hot magma heats the water. High pressure deep underground stops the water from boiling, even though it can reach 355°F (180°C) or more. The superhot water dissolves rock minerals.

Magma

Geyser

Sometimes, hot water and steam become trapped in an underground hollow because they can't escape quickly enough through the vent above. The pressure builds up, until the water and steam suddenly erupt as a geyser.

There are only about **1,000 geysers** *in the world.*

Some geysers erupt every few minutes or hours. Others go years between eruptions.

Mud pot

As the water rises, it absorbs volcanic gases, that make it acidic. The acid in the water attacks the rock and turns it into mud. The mud bubbles out at the surface, forming a mud pot.

Rainbow pool Grand Prismatic Spring in Yellowstone is the largest hot spring in the US. The rainbow colors that ring the deep-blue water come from huge amount of microbes that grow around the edge of the pool.

Mineral terrace Minerals that have dissolved in hot-spring water can turn solid as the water cools, forming amazing structures. Over thousands of years, spectacular terraces of stepped pools have formed at Pamukkale in Turkey.

Bathing pools To escape the cold and heavy snow of winter, macaque monkeys have learned how to keep warm by bathing in the hot springs of a mountain valley in central Japan.

Some sinkholes open under flowing streams.

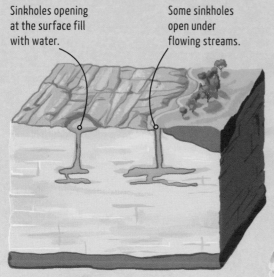

Carving cavities

As the trickling, flowing water eats away at the rock, the cracks widen and eventually become shafts and cavities beneath the surface.

Trickle down

Rain and water from streams find their way into cracks in limestone rock. The water slowly dissolves the rock and may carry away the minerals from which the rock is made.

Cave

Water is nature's sculptor, carving out spectacular caves and shaping weird rock formations underground. Rainwater absorbs carbon dioxide from the air as it falls and also from the soil as it seeps into the ground. The carbon dioxide turns the water into a very weak acid that is able to dissolve (break down) limestone and other rocks.

The world's longest cave system, Mammoth Cave in the US, stretches for at least 400 miles (640 km).

The water emerges from an opening at the base of the outcrop.

Escaping water

If the water can't go any deeper, it may wear away the rock near the base of the outcrop and create an escape route. The water emerges as a spring or as a stream that flows away.

The water makes its way to the ocean.

Getting larger

Over many thousands—even millions—of years, the action of the water enlarges the cavities, sometimes linking them together.

Blue holes

The most spectacular undersea caves formed long ago in limestone that was then above water. Rising sea levels later submerged the land. The "blue holes" that mark the cave entrances are collapsed sinkholes.

See also
Find out how rivers (26–27) are formed and how groundwater (30–31) gathers beneath land.

Emptying out

When the water finds an escape route, water levels fall and the cavities are emptied, forming caves or larger openings called caverns. The entire stream may now disappear underground.

Sea caves

Caves may form at the base of coastal cliffs as pounding waves force water into rock crevices. The rock eventually breaks up, creating caves that provide shelter for seals, seabirds, and other marine wildlife.

Stalactites and stalagmites may connect to form columns.

Stony sculptures

Mineral-rich water dripping from the cave roof evaporates, leaving behind tiny amounts of solid minerals. The minerals build up to create dangling, icicle-like stalactites, while "towers" called stalagmites form on the cave floor.

Ice caves

Water from melting ice sometimes carves out caves and tunnels in glaciers as it flows toward the ocean. Sunlight filtering through the ice gives the cave walls a beautiful blue shimmer.

A layer of water-resistant rock prevents the water from going deeper.

Volcanic island

Sometimes, a volcano erupts from the ocean floor and breaks through the ocean's surface to form a volcanic island. Over time, plants and animals appear on the island, and a coral reef may grow around it. Eventually, the volcano collapses back into the ocean.

Breaking the surface

If the eruption continues, the volcano eventually grows tall enough to break through the surface of the water. A new volcanic island is born. In tropical waters, coral grows and forms a reef around the shore, and plants colonize the land.

Above the surface of the water, the volcano continues to erupt.

Underwater eruption

A volcano erupts on the seabed when hot molten rock, called magma, breaks through a weak spot in Earth's crust. When the magma reaches the surface it is called lava. Over time, the lava builds up to create an underwater cone-shaped mountain.

See also
To find out more about volcanic activity under the water take a look at deep-sea vents (50–51).

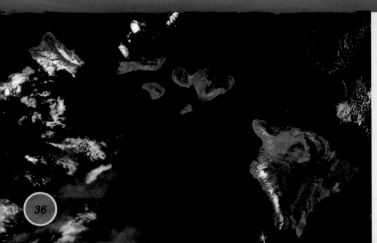

Hawaiian hot spot The Hawaiian Islands were formed over a hot spot under the Pacific Ocean. This hot spot is currently erupting to make the biggest and newest island in the southeast. Other islands of diminishing size were dragged away from this spot over millions of years.

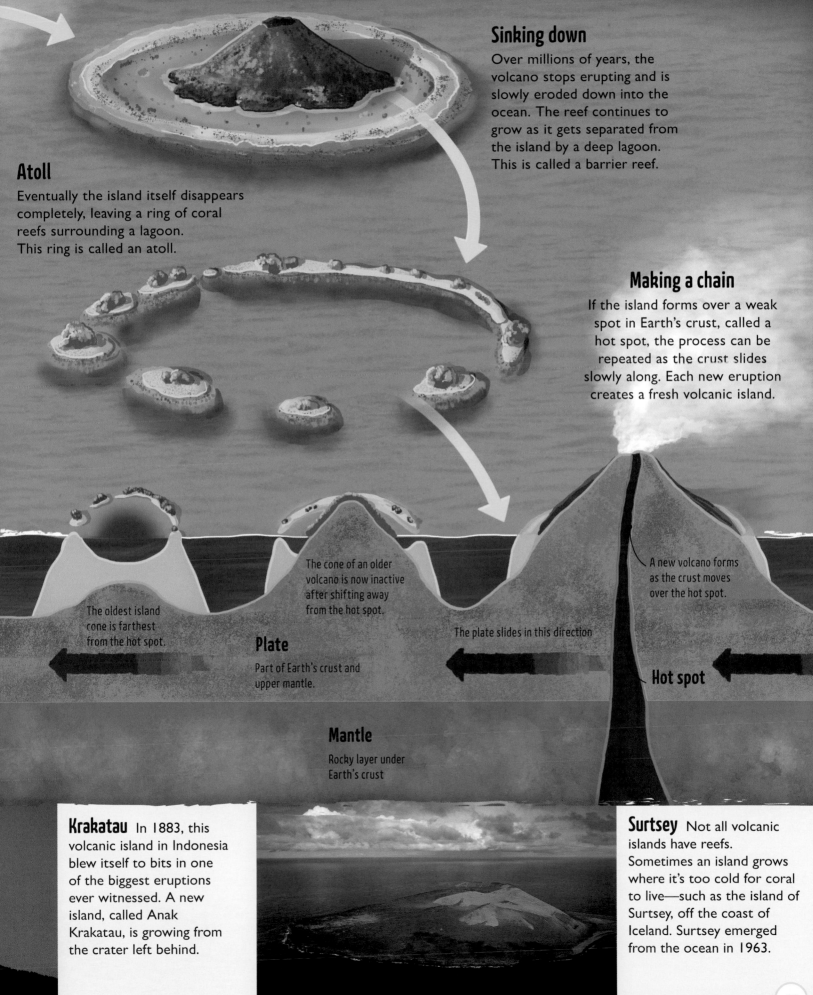

Sinking down

Over millions of years, the volcano stops erupting and is slowly eroded down into the ocean. The reef continues to grow as it gets separated from the island by a deep lagoon. This is called a barrier reef.

Atoll

Eventually the island itself disappears completely, leaving a ring of coral reefs surrounding a lagoon. This ring is called an atoll.

Making a chain

If the island forms over a weak spot in Earth's crust, called a hot spot, the process can be repeated as the crust slides slowly along. Each new eruption creates a fresh volcanic island.

A new volcano forms as the crust moves over the hot spot.

The cone of an older volcano is now inactive after shifting away from the hot spot.

The oldest island cone is farthest from the hot spot.

Plate

Part of Earth's crust and upper mantle.

The plate slides in this direction

Hot spot

Mantle

Rocky layer under Earth's crust

Krakatau In 1883, this volcanic island in Indonesia blew itself to bits in one of the biggest eruptions ever witnessed. A new island, called Anak Krakatau, is growing from the crater left behind.

Surtsey Not all volcanic islands have reefs. Sometimes an island grows where it's too cold for coral to live—such as the island of Surtsey, off the coast of Iceland. Surtsey emerged from the ocean in 1963.

See also

Learn how a snowflake (24–25) is formed.

Snowfall

Alpine glaciers begin high up in the mountains, where heavy snow falls in the winter. Gradually, the snow builds up into deep layers. This snow feeds the glacier.

Snow to ice

Over time, the snow gets buried under layer upon layer of fresh snowfall. Slowly, all the air trapped between the snowflakes gets squeezed out. This packed snow is called firn. Over many years, the firn itself turns to solid ice.

Snow

Firn

Glacial ice

Melting away

When the glacier reaches the lower slopes of a mountain, the ice begins to melt. The surface often looks dirty because sand and grit carried by the glacier is released by the melting ice. Huge cracks called crevices appear as the glacier slides over bumps in the rocks. The crevices can be more than 490 ft (50 m) deep.

Crevices

Moving downhill

The heavy ice slides downhill very, very slowly—usually about 10 in (25 cm) a day. The bottom layer of ice melts, helping the glacier to slide over the rock underneath. The ice scours the rock, chipping away small pieces, and carrying them along.

Glacier

High in the world's tallest mountain ranges and polar regions, there are vast rivers of ice called glaciers. They flow extremely slowly down slopes, scraping the landscape underneath. A glacier ends its life at the ocean, or it melts away on land and flows into streams.

Glacier's end

The end of a glacier is called the terminus (also called the toe or snout). When a glacier flows into a stream, pieces of ice break off and float away before melting. When the glacier flows into the ocean, massive chunks of ice break off and become icebergs floating in the water. This is called calving.

Ice sheets
Antarctica and Greenland are covered by thick layers of ice called ice sheets. The ice here is around 1¼ miles (2km) deep. The ice sheets feed glaciers that lead down to the ocean.

Glacial landscapes
Fjords are sea-filled valleys, gouged out by glaciers during cold periods in the past, called ice ages. During the ice ages, much of northern Europe and North America was covered with ice.

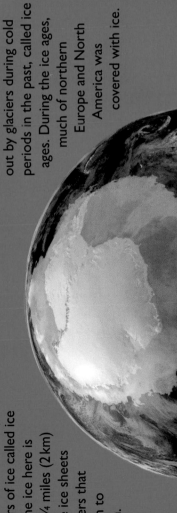

Ocean~surface currents

All through the world's oceans, there are invisible currents flowing. Some are tiny and local. Others are many times bigger than the Amazon, and flow for thousands of miles. They are driven mostly by the wind, and flow in giant loops around the largest oceans.

 The California Current flows south as part of the North Pacific Gyre. It carries cold water, making the climate cooler on the west coast of North America.

How currents start

Surface currents are created by the wind dragging on the surface of the water. They flow around each of the major oceans in giant loops called gyres. The currents don't flow in quite the same direction as the winds. Because Earth is spinning they curve away at angles. This makes currents veer right in the Northern Hemisphere, and left in the Southern Hemisphere.

North America

North Atlantic Gyre

North Pacific Gyre

South America

South Pacific Gyre

South Atlantic Gyre

Warm currents

Cold currents

Atacama Desert Cold eastern boundary currents can have a dramatic effect on the weather over the land. The cold water cools the air flowing over it and makes it very dry. The cold Humboldt Current off South America turns some regions into superdry deserts.

The Gulf Stream This strong, warm ocean current in the western North Atlantic is important because it helps make the weather in northwestern Europe much warmer than it would be otherwise. This is why palm trees can grow in the Scilly Isles in the UK.

The Gulf Stream flows northeast as part of the North Atlantic Gyre. It is a strong, warm ocean current that transports about 4 billion cubic feet (113 million cubic meters) of water per second.

 The Kuroshio Current is part of the North Pacific Gyre. This ocean current warms the southern part of Japan.

See also
Find out about deep-ocean currents (42–43) and waves (44–45).

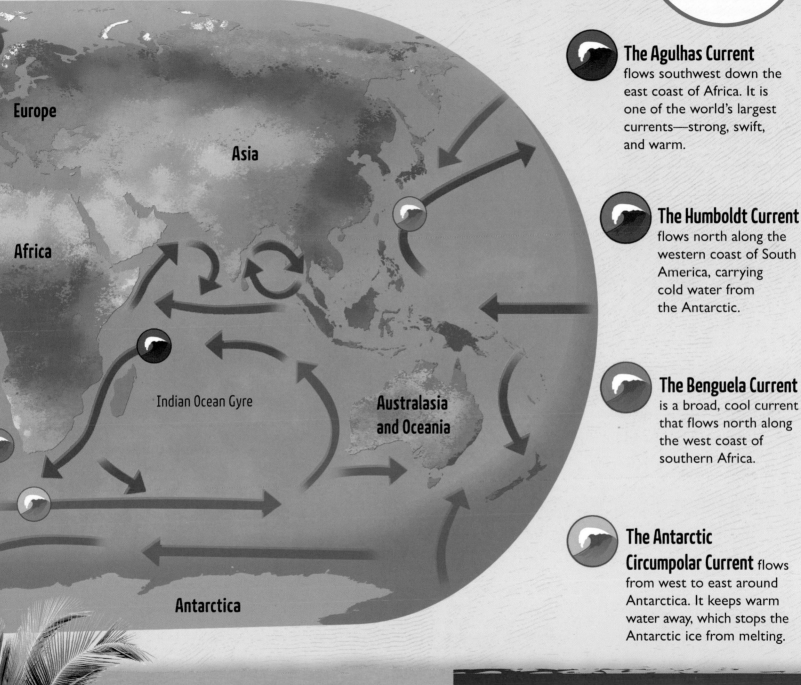

Europe

Asia

Africa

Indian Ocean Gyre

Australasia and Oceania

Antarctica

The Agulhas Current flows southwest down the east coast of Africa. It is one of the world's largest currents—strong, swift, and warm.

The Humboldt Current flows north along the western coast of South America, carrying cold water from the Antarctic.

The Benguela Current is a broad, cool current that flows north along the west coast of southern Africa.

The Antarctic Circumpolar Current flows from west to east around Antarctica. It keeps warm water away, which stops the Antarctic ice from melting.

The Kuroshio Current Located off the east coast of Japan, this ocean current can travel between 25-75 miles (40-120 kilometers) a day, and carries as much water as 6,000 large rivers. Its warm waters bring nutrients to the ocean off Japan, resulting in plentiful fishing there.

Icy start

In the chilly parts of the north Atlantic, some water gets so cold that it freezes. The water that doesn't freeze gets very salty and heavy. This heavy water then slips down to the ocean floor.

Deep~ocean currents

Deep down, the ocean is moving very slowly—so slowly, you can't see it happening. The amount of water moving, however, is huge! The whole ocean is gradually turning over like one huge conveyor belt, driven by variations in water density.

Southward bound

Down on the ocean floor, this dark, chilly water slides south through the Atlantic, pushed on by water sinking behind. Eventually it reaches as far south as Antarctica.

Stopping the conveyor Scientists are worried. When they study the waters south of Greenland, they see that the deep ocean conveyor is slowing down. Global warming stops the water from getting as cold. It also adds freshwater (from melting ice caps), which makes it less heavy. Without the push of heavy water to get the conveyor started, it might stop entirely. That might lead to more extreme climates around the world.

North again

The combined current flows on, south of Africa and back up through the Atlantic to complete the epic journey.

See also
Read about ocean-surface currents (40–41) and ocean waves (44–45).

Going up

As the cold water flows north again, it grows a little less salty and a little warmer. The water rises to the surface forming two vast currents that flow back west. They meet in the Indian Ocean, south of India.

Antarctic split

When it hits Antarctica, the water splits. One part creeps north under the Indian Ocean and another part travels east, right over to the Pacific.

Overturning water When plankton and other tiny sea creatures die, they sink beyond reach. In places where icy, cold water sinks, however, this pushes deep water up, carrying the rich food closer to the surface. Many whales migrate to Antarctica each year to dine on this food.

A long journey The great ocean conveyor takes a very long time to complete its journey. The water that is now arriving in Greenland probably began its journey from Greenland at the time the Vikings first arrived there in the 10th century!

Ocean waves

Ocean water is constantly on the move, in the form of waves. Some are gentle ripples that barely ruffle the surface. Others are mountains of water that can swamp the largest boat. They all start with the wind, which pushes the water as it blows across the ocean. The drag of the wind on the ocean surface is called wind stress.

Wave forming

Far out in the ocean, strong winds blow over the water's surface. As they blow, they whip the surface of the water into ripples. If the wind continues to blow, the ripples pile up into rolling waves.

The fetch

The water in a wave rotates, it does not go anywhere else.

Fetch and swell

The distance that the wind blows over the ocean is called the fetch. The longer the fetch, and the stronger the wind, the bigger the waves. In huge oceans, such as the Pacific and the Atlantic, the fetch can be so large that big, regular unbroken waves, called swell, build up. These swells can travel far across the ocean.

Rollers

Although the energy in waves travels far, the water in them just rolls around on the spot, creating up and down swells. Imagine a seabird floating on the surface that bobs up and down in one space, without moving forward.

Giant waves Storms can generate gigantic waves, though it is difficult to prove the height of the biggest waves. The largest officially recorded wave, however, is 112 ft (34 m), measured from the *USS Ramapo* in a hurricane in the Pacific in 1933.

*Teahupo'o, in Tahiti, has the world's **biggest**, most **dangerous** breakers.*

Surging breakers

On steep, sloping coasts, the waves surge and boom all of a sudden and fall back powerfully.

Spilling breakers

On gently sloping beaches, breaking waves rise up then spill softly far up on the beach.

Breakers

Eventually, the forward-leaning waves become unstable and spill over, crashing onto the shore as breakers.

Pile up

As waves reach shallower water near the coast, their bases catch on the bottom, but their tops keep speeding onward. This makes the waves pile up and lean forward.

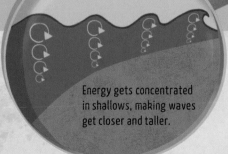

Energy gets concentrated in shallows, making waves get closer and taller.

See also
Read about ocean-surface currents (40–41) and deep-ocean currents (42–43).

Tsunami This is a series of waves generated by earthquakes and landslides. Most tsunamis travel along the seabed at high speed, then suddenly rear up as giant waves as they enter shallow water near the shore, with often devastating effects.

Surfing the waves

The people of Peru and Polynesia have been riding the ocean waves for thousands of years. Today, surfing is a global sport enjoyed by more than 25 million people.

Changing coastlines

Coastlines are places where the land meets the ocean or the sea, and they are constantly changing. Every few seconds, waves hit the shore, wearing away the land or reworking it into new shapes. Also, human activity has made our planet get warmer. As the world warms, ice caps and glaciers have melted, filling the oceans with more water. This has caused sea levels to rise, with even more impact on our coasts.

Sliding away

Cliffs may look mighty, but sometimes huge chunks of them slide into the water. Rain sinks into soil, gravel, and rock at the top of a cliff, making the ground heavier. Waves crash against the cliff, making it weaker. Over time, the cliff becomes weaker still, until eventually it collapses, sending soil and rock down into the water.

Caves, arches, and stacks

A headland is a piece of rocky land that sticks out into the ocean. As wind and water hit it, the rock is carved into different shapes. Caves are made when waves wear away cracks in the cliff face. A cave might break through to the other side of the land and form an arch. Some arches keep growing until they cannot support themselves. They then collapse, creating a pillar of rock called a stack.

Cave

Arch

Stack

White cliffs made of chalk are gradually worn away by wind and rain.

Direction of longshore drift

Sand movement

Wind direction

Beach on the move

The wind drives waves to break onto the shore at a particular angle. The waves carry sand and gravel onto the beach. As the waves retreat, they pull sand back too. Over time the sand is moved along the beach in a zigzag pattern and can end up being deposited farther down the shore. This is called longshore drift.

*About half of the world's human population lives on, or within **60 miles (100 km)** of, a coastline.*

Land underwater

Every year, the sea level rises by about 0.3 in (3.2 mm). Even a small increase can cause large areas of land to be covered with water. Over time, more and more people have been forced to move farther inland because their homes have been flooded.

Keeping the water back

Seawalls are built along the shore to protect land from being worn away by the waves. The walls might also help protect streets or buildings. Seawalls, however, are expensive to build and can stop wildlife from roaming along the coast.

First high tide

Because Earth spins, this harbor has two high tides and two low tides each day. At high tide, the ocean level is at its greatest height. Boats float easily, and coastal animals move around and feed, unseen, below the water's surface.

First low tide

Around six hours after high tide, the ocean is at its lowest level. Our boat is grounded and there is a lot of sand for making sand castles. Many coastal animals have moved to deeper water or are hiding in tide pools until the tide comes in again.

Tides

Where Earth faces the moon, gravity pulls the ocean into a bulge called a high tide. On the other side of the planet, the ocean is flung out into a second high-tide bulge. Between the bulges, sea levels fall, causing low tides.

Animals exposed at low tide may just have to sit tight, and wait for the water to return.

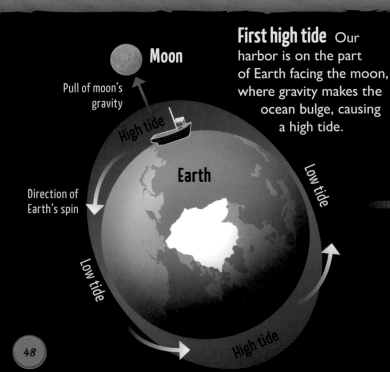

Moon

Pull of moon's gravity

High tide

Direction of Earth's spin

Low tide

Earth

Low tide

High tide

First high tide Our harbor is on the part of Earth facing the moon, where gravity makes the ocean bulge, causing a high tide.

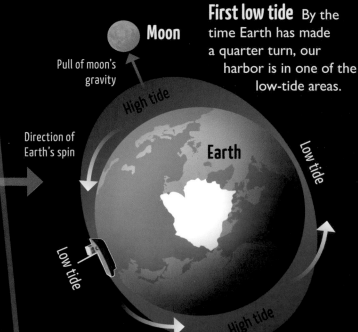

Moon

Pull of moon's gravity

High tide

Direction of Earth's spin

Low tide

Earth

Low tide

High tide

First low tide By the time Earth has made a quarter turn, our harbor is in one of the low-tide areas.

Second high tide

About another six hours later, the ocean level has risen once again. In some places, high tides are the same height, but in others they are slightly different. Anglers are trying to catch fish that swam back into the harbor.

Second low tide

In another six hours, it is low tide again. The boat is grounded once again and, since it is still light, birds are taking the opportunity to feed along the shore, catching prey revealed by the retreating tide or hidden in the sand.

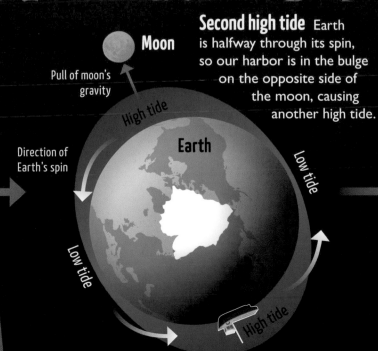

See also
Find out about different types of ocean waves (44–45).

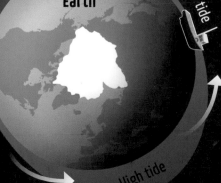

Second high tide Earth is halfway through its spin, so our harbor is in the bulge on the opposite side of the moon, causing another high tide.

Moon

Pull of moon's gravity

High tide

Direction of Earth's spin

Earth

Low tide

Low tide

High tide

Second low tide With Earth three-quarters of the way through its spin, the harbor passes through the second low-tide area.

Moon

Pull of moon's gravity

High tide

Direction of Earth's spin

Earth

Low tide

Low tide

High tide

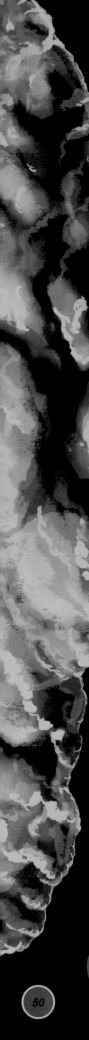

Deep-sea vent

In the dark ocean depths, jets of hot water spurt through cracks in the seabed. Called hydrothermal vents, they are a bit like underwater geysers. The water jets are intensely hot and full of dissolved minerals. Amazingly, life thrives in the harsh conditions around the vents, far beyond the reach of sunlight.

The jet that gushes from the top of the chimney looks like a plume of smoke. It can be black or white, depending on the mineral specks in the smoky clouds.

Growing chimneys

When the hot jet mixes with the nearly freezing ocean water, some of the dissolved minerals turn solid. The minerals settle on the seabed or build up to form tall "chimneys."

Vent chimneys can be up to 180ft (55 m) high.

Seeping down

Hydrothermal vents form in volcanic parts of the seabed, where the cold water of the deep ocean seeps down through cracks and crevices in the rocks of Earth's crust.

See also
Learn how magma also heats underground water to form hot springs and geysers (32–33).

Vent life

Bacteria and other microbes, called archaea, use the minerals in the hot jets to release the energy that they need to live. The microbes provide food for many animals that live around the vents.

Huge, red-gilled tube worms, nearly 6 ft (2 m) long, cluster around some chimneys.

More cold water seeps down to replace the water that is ejected.

Magma

Bursting out

Heat and pressure force the mineral-rich water back upward. It finds its way through more cracks and crevices and bursts through the sea floor as a scalding jet.

Heating up

As the water is heated by molten rock, or magma, welling up from inside Earth, it dissolves minerals from the crust. The water becomes superhot, but the immense pressure stops it boiling.

Vent communities In addition to tube worms, animals that live around vents may include mussels, crabs, shrimp, anemones, and even fish. Each year, new vent species are discovered, all adapted to life in this extreme habitat.

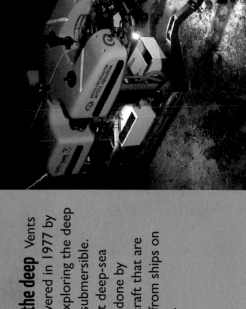

Exploring the deep Vents were discovered in 1977 by scientists exploring the deep ocean in a submersible. Today, most deep-sea research is done by uncrewed craft that are controlled from ships on the surface.

Using water

Water supports all life on Earth, from animals and plants to tiny organisms. It makes up about 70 percent of any living thing. Life's vital processes—such as photosynthesis in plants, and digestion in animals—rely on water. Water travels into, through, and out of our bodies. It is then recycled and used by other living things.

Water in cells

Living things are made of tiny living parts called cells. A cell is like a factory, with machines doing jobs inside, and things continually coming in and going out. Every cell has an important job to do, and all of the processes that take place within and around cells happen in water.

Animals drink to add water to their bodies and their cells.

Animal cell

The bodies of animals are finely balanced to ensure that they contain just the right amount of water. If their cells take in too much water, the cells might swell up, and their delicate cell membrane may split.

Cell membrane

Water enters the cell by osmosis

Nucleus

Cytoplasm

Gaining water

When water enters the body of an animal or a plant, it passes inside their cells by osmosis. This involves water seeping across a membrane toward a place with a higher concentration of dissolved substances. The cells absorb water by osmosis because they are surrounded by a cell membrane and contain dissolved substances such as concentrated salts and sugars.

An upright plant has firm, water-filled cells that allow it to stand tall and not droop.

Plant cell

Unlike in animals, the cells of plants are encased in a tough wall that overlies their cell membrane. This means when they take water in, their cells swell and get firm without bursting, which helps the plant stand upright.

Water enters the cell by osmosis

Cytoplasm

Vacuole stores most of the water inside a plant cell

Chloroplast makes food by photosynthesis

Cell wall

Cell membrane

Nucleus instructs cell what to do

Animal cell

Cytoplasm

Cell membrane

Nucleus

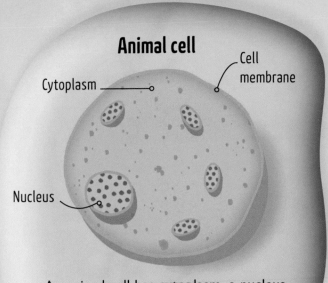

An animal cell has cytoplasm, a nucleus, and a membrane, but lacks a vacuole, chloroplasts, and a wall.

Animal cell

If animal cells lose water, they shrivel up.

Dogs don't sweat to cool down, instead they cool by losing water that evaporates from their airways when they pant.

Cells in balance

If the cells of an animal or a plant are surrounded by water with the same concentration of substances as inside the cells, osmosis does not happen. This means they neither gain nor lose water across their cell membranes, so their cells do not swell up or shrivel.

Losing water

When the body of an animal or plant gets dehydrated, water is lost from around the cells, and this raises the concentration of substances so it gets higher than inside the cells. This means water now seeps out of the cells across the cell membranes by osmosis.

Plants lose water through holes in their leaves when water evaporates. A plant wilts when the cells lose their firmness.

Plant cell

The cell membrane lies against the cell wall.

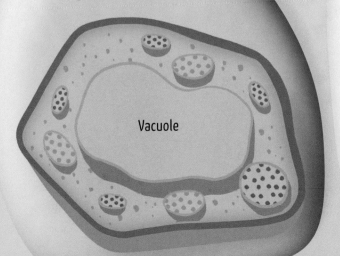

Vacuole

Plant cell

If plant cells lose water, their cell membrane pulls away from the cell wall as they shrivel up. Liquid from outside leaks into the space between the wall and the membrane.

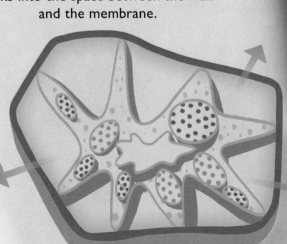

Making food

The leaves make food by using the sun's light energy to combine water in the leaves with carbon dioxide from the air. This chemical reaction makes sugar and other nutrients, and releases oxygen. A green pigment in the leaves called chlorophyll absorbs the sun's energy for this to happen.

Sunlight

Carbon dioxide

Water

Sugar

Oxygen

Transporting food

Water is added to the food made during photosynthesis. This sugary liquid is transported all around the plant in both directions through tubes called phloem vessels. This food gives the roots, stem, leaves, and flowers the energy they need to grow.

Sugar

See also
Read about how animals find food from water (58–59).

Stoma

Vein

Leaving the leaf

The sun warms the leaf and tiny holes called stomata open to let gases move in and out. The water in the leaf changes from a liquid to a gas and it evaporates out of the open stomata. As water leaves, it sucks more water up through the plant. The movement of water up through the xylem is called the transpiration stream.

Movement through a leaf

The xylem vessels carry water through the center of the leaf, and veins branch out to supply the rest of the leaf with water. It seeps into the surrounding leaf.

Water in plants

Plants need water to grow. Water in the soil seeps into roots, then travels up tubes that lead into the leaves, where it evaporates. Some of the water is used to make food in a process called photosynthesis, and some is held inside cells to keep them firm, helping the entire plant stay upright.

Movement up the stem

Xylem vessels are tubes arranged through the stem to carry water through the plant. Water is continually pulled up through the xylem vessels because water molecules stick together, so as water is lost from the leaves, it pulls more water up the stem.

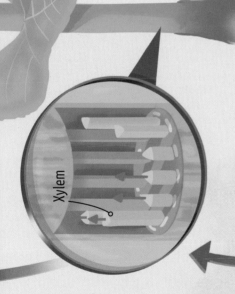

Xylem

Entering the roots

Each root has microscopic hairlike cells that reach into the soil, increasing the surface area of the roots to absorb water. Water enters the roots in a process called osmosis. The water travels through cells in the root and into tubes called xylem vessels.

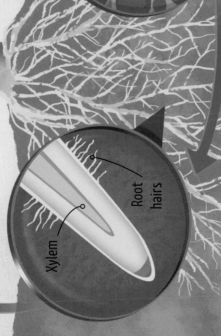

Xylem

Root hairs

Held in the soil

Water enters the soil when it rains. It moves through rocks and soil, dissolving them and collecting nutrients from the soil. Minerals from rocks and rotting material are dissolved in the water trapped between the soil particles.

Water

What makes plants wilt?

Plants start to wilt when they lose more water from their leaves than they gain through their roots. They lose the rigid structure the water supports. This can happen after several hot, dry days without rain.

Adaptation Mangroves live in saltwater. Their roots are adapted to filter out the salt from the water. The plants don't drown, and their succulent leaves have a waxy coating to minimize evaporation.

Desert plants Wide, thin leaves lose so much water by evaporation in hot, dry conditions that desert plants need to survive. To minimize the water lost from leaves in evaporation, cacti have thin spines. Their thick fleshy stems do the job of photosynthesis instead of leaves.

Food *from* water

Water has pressure, it can flow, and things float in it. Some living things use the ways that water behaves to help them find food. There are carnivorous, or meat-eating, plants that trap prey with water. Many animals that live attached to rocks or the seabed cannot move to search for food. Instead, they get their meals by trapping floating morsels carried by the water.

The common bladderwort lives in ponds, marshes, and streams. It has no roots, but takes in nutrients from water and the prey that it captures.

Pressure trap

The common bladderwort is a floating plant with balloonlike traps along its stems that catch prey such as insect larvae, water fleas, and aquatic worms. The traps, called bladders, use changes in water pressure to suck their victims in. When the trapdoor is shut, and the water inside the bladder is at a lower pressure than the water outside.

Antennae guide small prey to the trapdoor and keep animals too big to trap away from the trapdoor.

The trapdoor produces a sweet, slimy substance to attract prey.

Trigger hairs open the trapdoor when small prey touch them.

A water flea touches a trigger hair and the trapdoor springs open, sucking in water and the prey. The door shuts when the water pressure inside and outside the trap is the same.

Water always flows from areas of high pressure to low-pressure areas.

Chemicals called enzymes digest the victim. Water is then pumped out of the bladder, lowering the pressure inside. It is now ready to catch another meal.

Drowning pool

Like bladderworts, pitcher plants are carnivorous. They have a pitcher-shaped trap that holds water at the bottom. Insects feeding on sweet nectar at the rim lose their footing and tumble in. The victims drown, and enzymes in the water digest their soft body parts.

Insects slip on the trap's smooth, waxy surface.

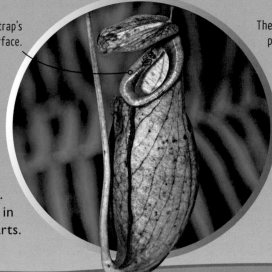

The pitchers of this pitcher plant develop on the end of long tendrils that grow from the tips of the plant's leaves.

Current collectors

Food carried in the current nourishes the Venus flytrap sea anemone and the predatory tunicate—two animals of the deep-ocean floor. Both animals face into the current and spread their trap wide, like a net, making a large area for collecting food.

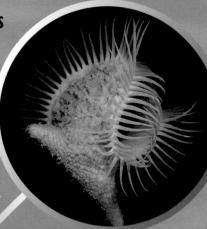

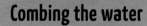

The tentacle-fringed flaps of the Venus flytrap sea anemone fold together to trap food items that land on them.

Feather stars are relatives of starfish. They spread their arms out to catch floating morsels of food.

The predatory tunicate eats food scraps and shrimp that the current washes into its gaping mouth.

Combing the water

Some animals of the shore and seabed use feathery limbs to collect food suspended, or hanging, in the water. They do this by waving their limbs back and forth, combing the water for food.

Filtering food

Many animals take water into their bodies and then strain out food particles or small animals as they expel the water. Filter feeders include bottom-dwelling animals such as sponges and clams, but also many fish and even some whales.

The inside of a sponge is lined with tiny beating hairs. The hairs pump water in and out of the sponge's body, straining particles of food from the water.

Water in humans

The Digestive System

Two-thirds of a human body is made from water. The organs and tissues that build a human are made from cells, and cells need water to work. Humans gain water by eating and drinking, and lose water through peeing, pooping, and sweating.

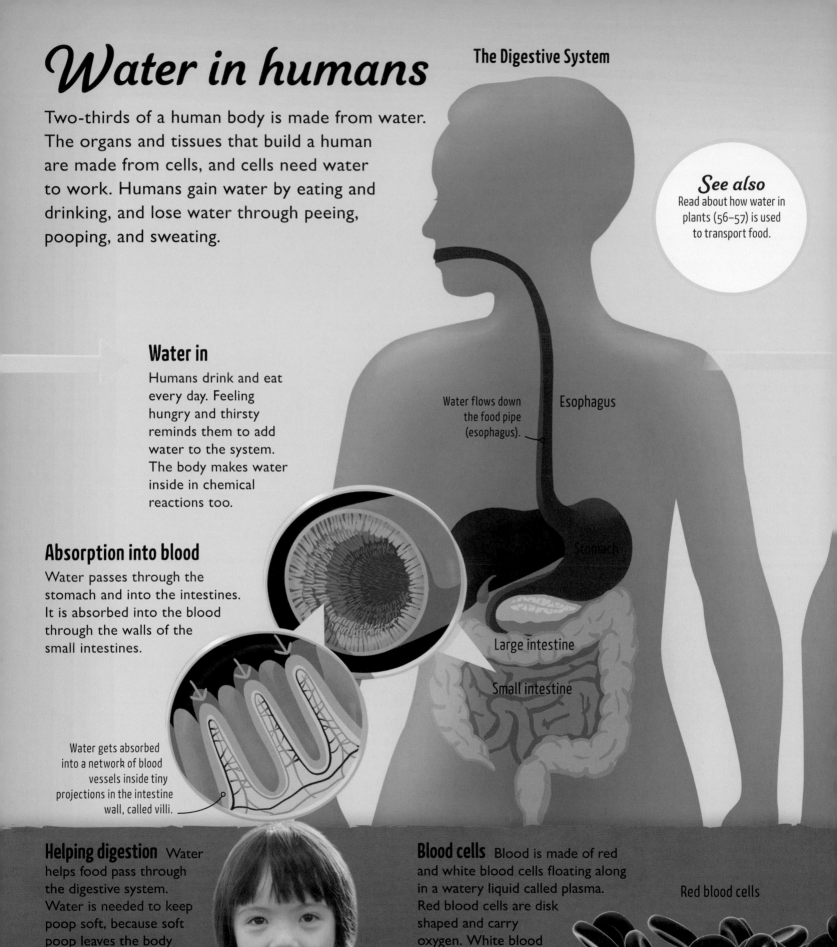

See also
Read about how water in plants (56–57) is used to transport food.

Water in

Humans drink and eat every day. Feeling hungry and thirsty reminds them to add water to the system. The body makes water inside in chemical reactions too.

Absorption into blood

Water passes through the stomach and into the intestines. It is absorbed into the blood through the walls of the small intestines.

Water flows down the food pipe (esophagus).

Esophagus

Stomach

Large intestine

Small intestine

Water gets absorbed into a network of blood vessels inside tiny projections in the intestine wall, called villi.

Helping digestion
Water helps food pass through the digestive system. Water is needed to keep poop soft, because soft poop leaves the body more smoothly than hard poop.

Blood cells
Blood is made of red and white blood cells floating along in a watery liquid called plasma. Red blood cells are disk shaped and carry oxygen. White blood cells fight bacteria and viruses.

Red blood cells

The Circulatory System

Carried in the blood

Blood is a mixture of cells floating in a liquid called plasma. Plasma is mostly made of water, and it has chemicals dissolved in it. The heart pumps blood around the body in tubes called blood vessels.

Heart

Water from blood collects between the cells before entering them.

Absorption into cells

Blood supplies organs and tissues in the body with water, food, and oxygen. Blood pressure caused by the pumping heart makes some of the water, and the chemicals it carries, squeeze out of the blood and into the cells.

The Excretory System

Watery sweat evaporates from the skin. Water also evaporates into the air from the lungs and airways.

Producing urine

Chemical waste produced by cells enters the blood and circulates to the kidneys. These organs filter the blood, so the waste is removed in water as a liquid called urine. Tubes called ureters fill the bladder with urine and when it's full, we urinate.

Kidneys

Ureters

Bladder

Perspiration Sweating helps the body cool down. Sweat is made in glands in the skin. As sweat leaves the skin, it turns from liquid to vapor, or evaporates, taking heat away from the body.

Surviving dehydration

Camels can travel for several days without drinking or eating in the deserts where they live. The dromedary camel survives in the hot, dry Sahara desert with a hump that stores energy as fat and a body that can tolerate extreme temperatures and dehydration.

Dehydrated blood vessels get narrower, and blood cells shrink to flat ovals so they can still flow through the blood vessels.

Time to eat

Camels can survive by eating dry plants that are low in nutrients. They chew tough food then swallow and bring it back up to chew again to extract as many of these nutrients as possible.

Blood cells can swell to more than twice their size without bursting as they absorb water.

Camels graze on desert plants to gain water and energy whenever they can.

Hydrated blood

The gut slowly releases water into the blood, which stops the blood from getting too diluted too quickly. The wafer-thin blood cells then puff up to more than two times their normal size as water soaks into them.

Camel drinks

A camel typically drinks 2.5 to 5 gallons (10 to 20 liters) per minute, but this can reach up to 34.3 gallons (130 liters) per minute. This is far more than other animals can drink at one time.

Dehydrated camel

Most animals die if they lose more than 15 percent of the water in their body, but a camel can lose twice this amount and still be okay. As the camel loses water its blood loses water too.

Staying fueled

The fat in the camel's hump is burned up to release energy when the camel has little to eat. As the fat is used up, the hump gets floppy.

Resurrection plant

This desert plant looks shriveled up and dead with its brown leaves. After rain, the plant quickly absorbs water so it can unfurl and turn green again.

Keeping cool

The camel's body can tolerate a high temperature—and will only start to sweat when it gets really hot. This saves precious water.

The camel breathes slowly and deeply, to reduce water vapor lost when breathing out.

Rüppell's fox
The Rüppell's fox never drinks! This desert mammal hunts at night. It gains water from its food and from converting food to water within its body.

Camel kidneys

A camel's kidneys filter its blood, taking water and waste out as urine. When a camel is dehydrated, the kidneys keep water, making the urine more concentrated.

Bactrian camel
The bactrian camel, from Asia's Gobi desert, has a shaggy, thick coat to keep it warm in the winter, but it sheds it in the spring. It has adaptations similar to the dromedary camel.

See also
Find out how humans experience feeling thirsty (66–67), triggering a response to water.

Collecting water

In deserts and other dry places where it rarely rains, finding enough water to survive is difficult. Some living things have changed their bodies and behavior so that they can collect as much water as possible in these harsh habitats. Even a small amount of water can be the difference between life and death.

Drinking mist

This darkling beetle in Africa's Namib Desert drinks the early morning mist that blows in from the ocean. It faces the breeze and does a kind of handstand, raising its rear into the mist. Water droplets settle on the beetle's wing cases and run down into its mouth.

Fog collecting

The spines of a cactus not only protect against plant eaters, they also collect water droplets from desert fogs. The water runs along the spines to the stem and trickles down to the roots. In some cacti, the stem itself can absorb water.

Desert drinking

The thorny devil lizard of Australia uses its scaly skin to draw water from the ground. When the lizard presses its belly into damp sand, moisture is sucked up through tiny channels between the thorny devil's scales and pulled toward its mouth. It may also shovel sand onto its back to get even more water.

Water gets drawn in through the tiny spaces by a process called capillary action—just like a paper towel soaking up moisture.

Water travels along the body and into the thorny devil's mouth.

Groovy scales

To make the most of any rain, some rattlesnakes coil tightly and drink the water that collects on their scales. A maze of small grooves on the surface of the scales stops the water from running off and holds it there as droplets, which the snake laps up.

Taking water from air

To get water in the dry season, the Australian green tree frog cools off at night and then retreats into a burrow or tree hollow. Once inside, water condenses out of the warm air onto the frog's colder body—like the way droplets form on a cold bottle of water from the fridge.

The air in the burrow or hollow is warm and damp.

The frog absorbs water through its skin.

The bird collects water by rocking from side to side and shaking his belly feathers in the water. It can take 15 minutes to "fill up."

Water carrier

Sandgrouse chicks can feed themselves when they hatch, but the male parent brings them water to drink. He flies to a water hole and dunks his belly into the pool. His belly feathers have special feltlike feathers that can soak up four times more water than a sponge. Then he flies back to his thirsty chicks, carrying the water with him.

A male sandgrouse may fly a round trip of 75 miles (120 km) when collecting water for his chicks.

The chicks drink by squeezing the male's wet feathers with their beaks.

Feeling thirsty

The brain keeps track of fluid levels in the body. When water levels fall, the brain sends chemical signals to the rest of the body to make adjustments. The brain also causes you to feel thirsty, so you drink and rehydrate.

Fluids drop

When levels of water in the blood and other body fluids drop, it raises the blood's concentration. Cells in the brain detect this rise, and the brain makes you feel thirsty.

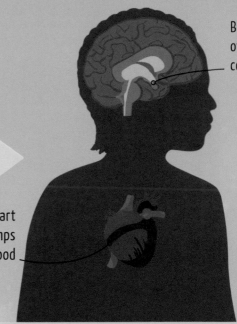

Brain keeps track of the blood's concentration

Heart pumps blood

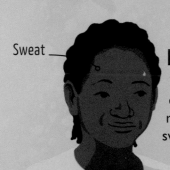

Sweat

Exercise

The body uses up water during exercise, and it releases heat. Humans sweat to draw heat away from the body to cool down.

See also
Read about how a camel survives dehydration (62–63) and how animals collect water (64–65).

Water intake

Drinking fluids keeps blood and cells hydrated so they can work properly. The amount of fluid you need depends on your body weight, how much exercise you do, and the weather, but as a rough guide here is the amount of water you need to drink every day. Consult with your pediatrician on how much fluid a child under the age of one needs.

Child 9–13 years old:
7–8 cups (1.6–1.9 liters)

Child 1–3 years old:
4 cups (0.9 liters) of fluids

Child 4–8 years old:
5 cups (1.1 liters)

Child 14–18 years old:
8–11 cups (1.9–2.6 liters)

Shades of urine
When we are dehydrated, the kidneys retain water so urine is less watery and more concentrated, becoming darker in color. When our body is hydrated, urine looks lighter because it's diluted with more water.

Salty foods
The salt in our food is absorbed into our blood and raises its salt concentration. This means it ends up affecting the brain and body in the same way as when we lose water—we feel thirsty and we pee less water.

Releasing a signal

These cells are in a part of the brain called the hypothalamus, which sits above a gland called the pituitary gland. The hypothalamus makes this gland release a chemical hormone.

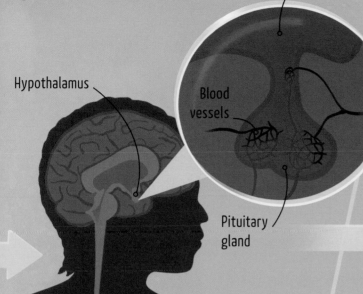

Hypothalamus

Base of hypothalamus

Blood vessels

Pituitary gland

Kidneys respond

The hormone circulates in the bloodstream until it reaches the kidneys. It makes the kidneys retain more water in the blood, so less water gets released in urine when you pee.

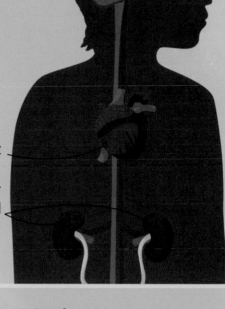

Brain

Heart

Kidneys filter blood

Men 19 years and over:
15.5 cups (3.7 liters)

Women 19 years and over:
11.5 cups (2.7 liters)

Pregnant women:
10 cups (2.3 liters)

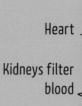

Drinking

It takes five minutes for water to start to enter the blood and about ten minutes for most of it to get through. We stop drinking sooner, however, thanks to the physical sensation of swallowing water. This sensation tells our brain we're no longer thirsty.

Bladder function Urine collects in a sac called the bladder. As this fills up, its walls stretch and send electrical signals to the brain so we know we need to pee. When we're ready to pee, we relax a ring of muscle to open the bladder and we contract muscles in the bladder wall to push urine out.

Life
in water

Life began in water billions of years ago.
Today, a rich variety of plants and animals still
make water their home—surviving, growing,
and reproducing on and beneath its surface.
From the deepest oceans to the tiniest ponds
and fastest rivers, aquatic life thrives all
over our planet.

Surviving in water

Living things that dwell in water must deal with very different conditions from those that spend their lives on land. Water is denser (thicker) than air, so it is harder to move through, and it also holds less oxygen than air. The bodies of aquatic organisms, combined with the way they live, are especially suited to their watery habitats.

Long, pointed, "streamlined" bodies help some animals move smoothly through water.

This albatross uses its webbed feet to paddle over the water's surface.

Moving along

It takes more energy to move through water than through air, especially for the tiniest creatures. Many aquatic animals swim by swishing their bodies from side to side. Others use body parts such as flippers to propel themselves along. The smallest animals, called zooplankton, travel by drifting with the current rather than struggling to swim against it.

For zooplankton, such as these copepods, swimming through water would be like us trying to swim through molasses.

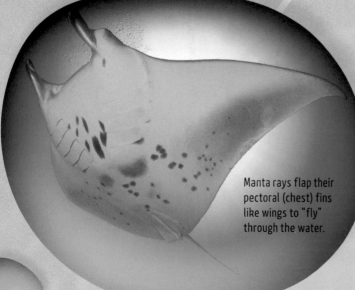

Manta rays flap their pectoral (chest) fins like wings to "fly" through the water.

Corals reproduce by releasing small bundles of sperm and eggs directly into the water.

The blue whale is the largest animal that has ever lived.

When washed ashore, the soft-bodied lion's mane jellyfish—the world's biggest jellyfish—cannot get back into the ocean.

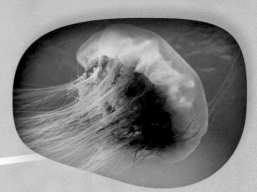

Growing bigger

Water supports bodies better than air does. So things that live in water can grow really big without needing especially strong skeletons (in animals) or supporting tissues like wood (in plants). That's why huge whales, big jellyfish, and giant seaweed become floppy and helpless when stranded on land.

Getting oxygen

Fish and many other aquatic creatures breathe using organs called gills, which absorb oxygen from the water. Mammals and reptiles that live in the water have lungs, not gills. Lungs take oxygen from the air, so these animals must come to the surface to breathe. Most amphibians have gills as aquatic young, then lungs as land-living adults.

Amphibians normally lose their gills when they become adults, but axolotls keep their pink, feathery gills throughout their lives.

In the polar winter, when the ocean freezes over, seals make breathing holes in the ice so that they can come up for air.

Making babies

Sperm need water to swim to eggs and fertilize them. Most animals that live in water release a lot of sperm and eggs, and rely on the chance that fertilization will happen. Some, however, take sperm into their bodies through mating, to make it more likely that their eggs will be fertilized.

When dolphins mate, the eggs are fertilized inside the female's body.

Ocean environments

From icy polar waters to warm tropical seas, and from the bright, wave-churned surface to the gloomy, high-pressure deep, conditions in the ocean vary greatly. Yet wherever they live, and at whatever depth, marine life has adapted to their local surroundings and successfully live, feed, and breed.

Tropical waters

In the tropics, which lie around the middle of Earth, the sun is almost directly overhead all year round. Tropical seas are always warm. The coral reefs that grow in shallow tropical waters provide a habitat for all kinds of colorful marine life.

Polar seas

Though ice covers the ocean around the North and South Poles in winter, polar waters are rich in nutrients. Polar mammals, such as seals, and birds, such as penguins, keep the cold out with fatty blubber. Fish in polar waters have chemicals in their bodies that stop them from freezing.

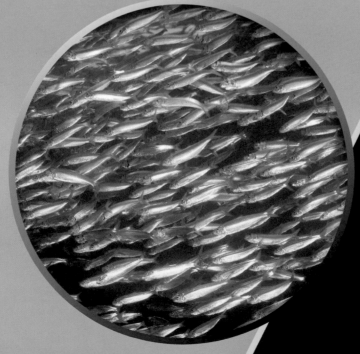

Temperate seas

Between the chilly poles and the warm tropics are cool, temperate seas. Large schools of fish, such as sardines, herring, and anchovies, cruise the open ocean in search of small crustaceans to eat. The schools are preyed on by larger fish, marine mammals, and seabirds.

The deepest place is the Mariana Trench, in the western Pacific, which plunges to 36,200 ft (11,030 m).

The deepest places are where the ocean's floor drops away, forming chasms called ocean trenches.

Turtle

Animals of the sunlit zone include many species of fish, turtles, and mammals such as whales and dolphins.

Sunlit zone

Most ocean organisms live in bright, sunlit waters near the surface, where tides, currents, and winds keep the ocean in motion, and where the temperature changes with the seasons. Plankton, made up of tiny, plantlike algae and small creatures, provides food for a host of marine animals. Animals that feed on plankton are in turn hunted by larger predators.

0–660 ft (0–200 m)

Dolphin

Jellyfish

In the dim twilight zone, animals often have large, extrasensitive eyes to collect as much light as possible.

Hatchetfish

Twilight zone

There is just enough light in the twilight zone for animals to see, but not enough for algae to survive. Many twilight animals swim up to the surface at night to feed, then swim back down by day. Others stay put and ambush prey using huge jaws and teeth. Some twilight animals make light to confuse predators, find mates, or lure prey.

660–3,300 ft (200–1,000 m)

Snipe eel

Shark

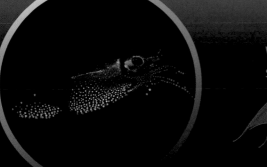

Vampire squid

Midnight zone

In the eerie deep, it is utterly dark, very cold, and the weight of the water above presses with huge force on the animals that live there. A lot of animals in the midnight zone can make their own light, but others are blind and find food and mates using hearing and touch, and by detecting scents and movements in the water.

3,300–19,700 ft (1,000–6,000 m)

Making light

Many animals that live in the dim and dark depths can flash or glow with light. This is because their bodies contain pockets of bacteria that can make light from chemicals. Scientists call this bioluminescence, which means "light from living things."

Humpback anglerfish

Some deep-ocean animals feed on decaying particles that fall like snow from above.

Sea pigs

Life *in* water

Earth formed about 4.5 billion years ago. At some point, a single ocean may have covered the surface of the young Earth. Water provided the right conditions for life to begin. At the beginning, and for about 3 billion years, life was just madeup of single-celled microbes far too small to be seen with the unaided eye.

Animals

The earliest animals were soft-bodied creatures. Some stayed attached to the seabed and absorbed nutrients from the water. Others crawled along, feeding on nutrients on the seabed.

Jets of water escaping from deep-sea vents contain minerals from underground rocks.

Oxygen producers

Some microbes in sunlit shallow waters could photosynthesize—collecting light and changing it into energy that they could use. As they did this, they released the gas oxygen, which is why the oceans and atmosphere are rich in this gas today.

Although it looked like a fern, Charnia was an animal that lived on the deep-ocean floor.

Multicelled life

Most microbes were poisoned by all the extra oxygen. But, others thrived and gradually developed into new life forms, some of which were bigger and made up of many cells. Algae appeared, including the first seaweeds.

Life begins

Life possibly began where cracks in the deep-ocean floor, called hydrothermal vents, gushed hot, mineral-rich water. The earliest single-celled microbes got their energy by absorbing minerals from the water.

Blue-green cyanobacteria were among the first microbes that could photosynthesize.

The first seaweeds were much larger than microbes but still just a few millimeters long.

4
bya

600
mya

bya = billion years ago
mya = million years ago

3.5
bya

1
bya

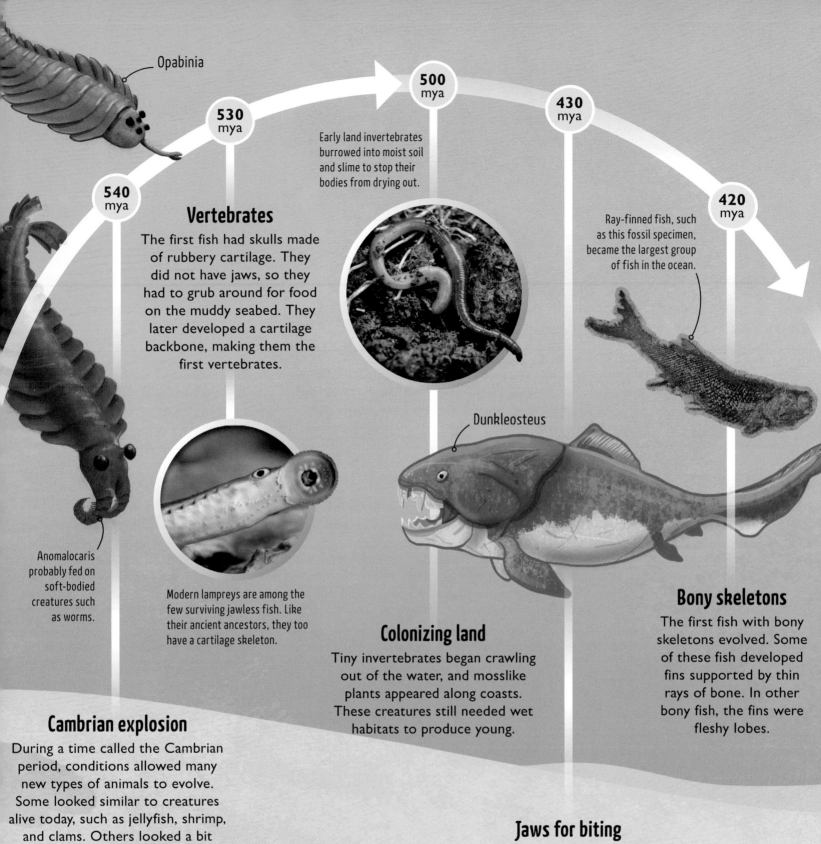

Opabinia

500
mya

530
mya

430
mya

540
mya

Early land invertebrates burrowed into moist soil and slime to stop their bodies from drying out.

420
mya

Ray-finned fish, such as this fossil specimen, became the largest group of fish in the ocean.

Vertebrates

The first fish had skulls made of rubbery cartilage. They did not have jaws, so they had to grub around for food on the muddy seabed. They later developed a cartilage backbone, making them the first vertebrates.

Dunkleosteus

Anomalocaris probably fed on soft-bodied creatures such as worms.

Modern lampreys are among the few surviving jawless fish. Like their ancient ancestors, they too have a cartilage skeleton.

Bony skeletons

The first fish with bony skeletons evolved. Some of these fish developed fins supported by thin rays of bone. In other bony fish, the fins were fleshy lobes.

Colonizing land

Tiny invertebrates began crawling out of the water, and mosslike plants appeared along coasts. These creatures still needed wet habitats to produce young.

Cambrian explosion

During a time called the Cambrian period, conditions allowed many new types of animals to evolve. Some looked similar to creatures alive today, such as jellyfish, shrimp, and clams. Others looked a bit like space aliens!

Jaws for biting

Some fish evolved jaws, so they could now bite and tackle larger pieces of food. Many jawed fish, including Dunkleosteus, belonged to a group of armor-plated predators called placoderms.

Hallucigenia

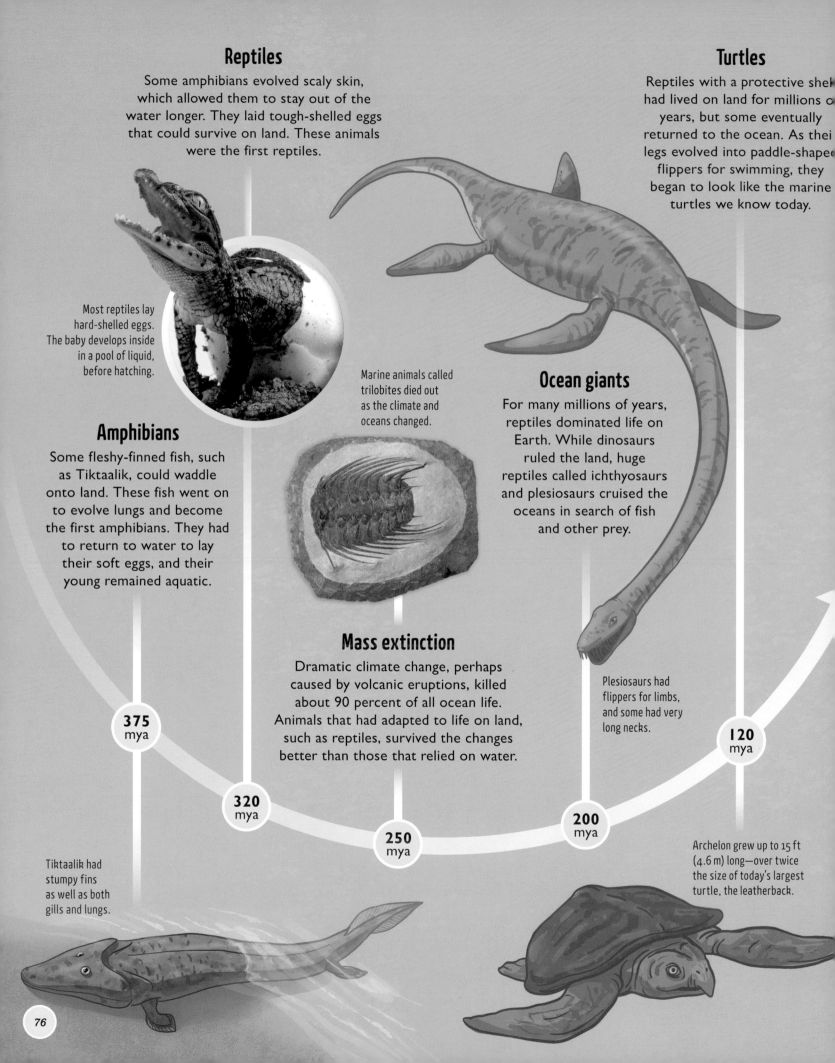

Reptiles

Some amphibians evolved scaly skin, which allowed them to stay out of the water longer. They laid tough-shelled eggs that could survive on land. These animals were the first reptiles.

Most reptiles lay hard-shelled eggs. The baby develops inside in a pool of liquid, before hatching.

Turtles

Reptiles with a protective shel had lived on land for millions o years, but some eventually returned to the ocean. As thei legs evolved into paddle-shape flippers for swimming, they began to look like the marine turtles we know today.

Amphibians

Some fleshy-finned fish, such as Tiktaalik, could waddle onto land. These fish went on to evolve lungs and become the first amphibians. They had to return to water to lay their soft eggs, and their young remained aquatic.

Marine animals called trilobites died out as the climate and oceans changed.

Ocean giants

For many millions of years, reptiles dominated life on Earth. While dinosaurs ruled the land, huge reptiles called ichthyosaurs and plesiosaurs cruised the oceans in search of fish and other prey.

Mass extinction

Dramatic climate change, perhaps caused by volcanic eruptions, killed about 90 percent of all ocean life. Animals that had adapted to life on land, such as reptiles, survived the changes better than those that relied on water.

Plesiosaurs had flippers for limbs, and some had very long necks.

375 mya

320 mya

250 mya

200 mya

120 mya

Tiktaalik had stumpy fins as well as both gills and lungs.

Archelon grew up to 15 ft (4.6 m) long—over twice the size of today's largest turtle, the leatherback.

100
mya

66
mya

60
mya

50
mya

Today

Impact!

When a huge asteroid struck Earth, it covered the planet with dust and cooled the world. The dinosaurs soon became extinct, as did the ichthyosaurs and plesiosaurs, and many other animals.

Dust caused by the impact blocked out the sun. Cold, dark conditions lasted for many years.

Marine mammals

Small land mammals survived the asteroid impact. They thrived because there were no large reptiles to prey on them. Many grew larger, and some adapted to life in the water, evolving into marine mammals, such as whales, seals, and manatees.

Some whales evolved bristly baleen, which replaced teeth, for filtering food from the water.

Crocodiles

The earliest ancestors of crocodiles were reptiles that lived on land and walked upright on two legs. Later, however, crocodilians took to the water. A few ancient relatives of today's crocs even lived entirely at sea.

This huge megalodon tooth is shown with the tooth of today's great white shark.

Modern crocodiles and alligators are survivors of the reptile group called archosaurs, which includes dinosaurs, birds, and flying pterosaurs.

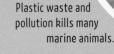
Plastic waste and pollution kills many marine animals.

Rise of sharks

Sharks survived the mass extinction. Now that the large ocean reptiles were gone, sharks thrived to become the new big ocean predators. Some, such as megalodons, may have grown up to 60 ft (18 m) long.

Oceans at risk

Today, human actions threaten ocean life. Building on coastlines is destroying ocean habitats, while global warming is melting glaciers and polar ice, raising sea temperatures, and making the ocean more acidic.

Spawning jellyfish

Swarms of moon jellies gather near the coast to spawn. The male releases sperm into the water, which the female collects with her frilly oral arms. She takes the sperm inside her body to fertilize her eggs.

Sex organs

Sperm

Oral arms

The medusa swims by pulsing water in and out of its bell to push itself through the water.

Bell

Full moon

The moon jelly is now an adult medusa. It stings prey with its tentacles and pulls the victims into its mouth using its oral arms. The mouth is also where the jellyfish gets rid of undigested waste.

Stinging tentacles

Jellyfish

Looking like an ocean ghost with its see-through body, the moon jelly is one of the most common types of jellyfish and lives in coastal waters around the world. For just a short time, it lives as a free-swimming, bell-shaped jellyfish or "medusa." It spends much more of its life attached to the seabed.

The larvae are weak swimmers, so they mostly float and drift as part of the plankton.

Young jellies

The female keeps the fertilized eggs on her oral arms. She releases them when they have developed into larvae. Each larva swims by beating tiny hairs called cilia, and it lives among microscopic plankton for a while.

Breaking away

The polyp's top segment peels off and swims away as a baby jellyfish. This continues until all the segments are gone. The polyp is left behind on the seabed, and continues living for up to two decades.

As the young jellyfish grows, it looks more and more like its parents.

The polyp uses its tentacles to reach up into the water and catch prey.

Tentacled polyp

Eventually, the moon jelly larva settles on the seabed and attaches itself to rock, coral, or another solid surface. Now called a polyp, its body becomes stalklike, with little tentacles around the mouth at the top.

Making copies

When conditions are right, the polyp reproduces asexually (without mating) by making copies of itself. It loses its tentacles, grows longer, and its body divides into segments that will become baby jellyfish.

The polyp's body now looks like a stack of miniature bowls.

See also

Read about other creatures of the ocean, such as the clown fish (106–107) and the starfish (90–91).

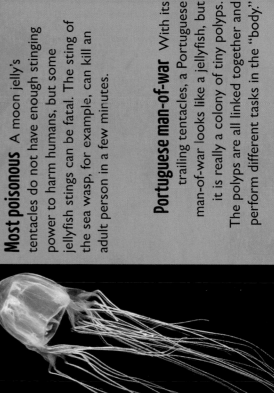

Most poisonous A moon jelly's tentacles do not have enough stinging power to harm humans, but some jellyfish stings can be fatal. The sting of the sea wasp, for example, can kill an adult person in a few minutes.

Portuguese man-of-war With its trailing tentacles, a Portuguese man-of-war looks like a jellyfish, but it is really a colony of tiny polyps. The polyps are all linked together and perform different tasks in the "body."

Never say die

A jellyfish medusa usually lives for just a few months. But some species are known as immortal jellyfish because their medusae can turn back into polyps and start that part of their life cycle all over again.

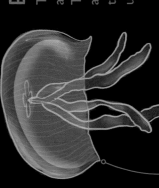

Fluke

Parasites are creatures that live on, or in, the body of another species, called the host. A fluke is a type of parasite. One kind of fluke first infects a freshwater snail, then a tadpole, and lastly a bird. The fluke reproduces twice during its life cycle, first sexually, by mating, and then asexually, without mating.

Inside the bird

The bird digests the frog's body, releasing the parasites, which settle in the bird's gut. Here they develop into adults, ready to mate and start the cycle all over again.

No escape

Frogs with too many or too few legs cannot swim or jump properly, and are less able to escape predators. They are easy prey for birds such as hawks and herons, which pluck them from the water.

Hawks fly low over the water and snatch the helpless frogs.

Egg release

Adult flukes mate while living in the gut of a bird. Their fertilized eggs are released into the water in the bird's droppings.

See also

To find out more about life in water take a look at the time line pages (74–77).

Finding a new host

The eggs hatch into free-swimming larvae. Each larva searches until it finds a new host—this time, it is a freshwater snail. The larva enters the snail's body through the skin.

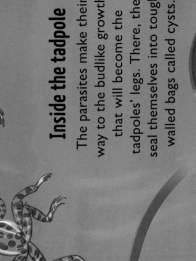

The water breaks up the bird's droppings and the eggs float free.

The larva swims by beating tiny hairs called cilia.

Interfering cysts

As the tadpole changes into a frog, the cysts interfere with the growth of the young frog's legs. The frog may not grow enough legs, or it may sprout extra legs that stick out at weird angles.

Inside the tadpole

The parasites make their way to the budlike growths that will become the tadpoles' legs. There, they seal themselves into tough-walled bags called cysts.

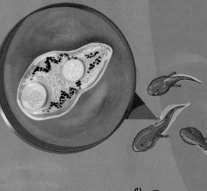

Inside the snail

The larva now takes on a wormlike shape. It reproduces asexually— without its eggs needing to be fertilized. This allows it to produce hundreds or thousands of babies on its own.

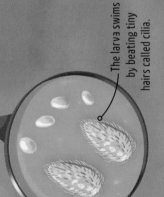

Tadpole target

Some of the babies stay inside the snail and themselves become "mothers." Others, with tails, leave the snail and swim off to infect their next host—a tadpole.

False tongue
The tongue-eating louse is a parasitic crustacean that eats the tongue of a fish. It then attaches itself to the stub of the tongue and lives in the mouth, feeding on the fish's blood and mucus.

Eye eater
One parasitic crustacean lives attached to the eye of a shark. It feeds on the eye tissue and harms the shark's ability to see. Luckily, the shark relies more on smell than sight, so it can still hunt prey.

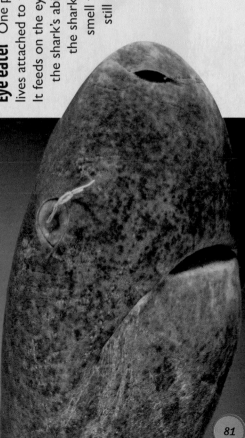

Periwinkle

Often spotted on rocks and in small pools of water at the seaside, the edible periwinkle's life is closely linked with the rhythm of the tides. This marine snail, a type of mollusk, grazes on algae growing on the rocks. It starts life in the plankton, before making its home on the shore.

The high tides give the slow-moving snails more time for mating.

Mating underwater

In spring, edible periwinkles mate underwater at night, and at especially high tides that occur when there is a full or new moon. The male's sperm fertilizes eggs inside the female's body.

The female leaves a scent in her trail of slime to attract mates.

Egg capsules

An hour later, while still underwater at the same high tide, the female releases capsules holding fertilized eggs. She stores some sperm in her body and continues to release eggs at other full and new moon tides.

There are usually two or three eggs in each capsule.

The larvae swim using flaps lined with beating hairs.

Bursting free

The egg capsules float among the plankton. They absorb water and swell, and after several days they burst. Tiny, free-swimming larvae (young) hatch from the eggs.

Live bearer
The female rough periwinkle does not release eggs but gives birth to live babies. The eggs hatch and grow in a special pouch inside her, and when the babies emerge they are fully formed little sea snails.

Toughest teeth
Like periwinkles, limpets have toothed tongues for feeding on algae. Their teeth are made of the hardest material in the animal world. Limpets leave trails of scratches on rocks as they graze.

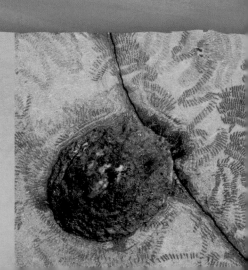

Grown-up

By winter, the periwinkles are fully adult, and they will be able to breed when spring comes. If they are not eaten by hungry birds, crabs, or fish, the periwinkles can live between five and ten years.

The periwinkle's hard shell gives it some protection, but a green crab can crush it with its pincers.

Hanging on

After one or two months, the larvae are carried ashore by waves that crash onto the rocks. Only those that manage to attach to the rocks with their muscular foot will survive.

When out of the water at low tide, the periwinkles sit tight, locked into their shells.

See also
A periwinkle's life is affected by tides. Find out more about how tides (48–49) work.

Larvae washed into rock crevices have the best chance of hanging on.

Life between the tides

Now strong enough to withstand the waves, the periwinkles emerge from the shelter of rock crevices. They breathe through gills as they creep around and feed underwater at high tide.

Periwinkles scrape food off submerged rocks with their toothed tongues.

Low-tide blob The beadlet anemone (left) is another seaside animal. To stop its body from drying out when exposed to the air at low tide, it makes itself smaller by pulling its tentacles in, so that it looks like a blob of red jello (right).

Killifish

Some tropical killifish live for just a short time in pools that form during the rainy season. They grow quickly, mate, then lay their eggs. When the dry season comes, the adults die but the eggs remain alive, sealed in dried mud, ready to hatch when the rains return.

Brine shrimp

Brine shrimp can live in salt lakes with water over ten times saltier than the ocean. If the water becomes too salty even for the brine shrimp, the females lay eggs with protective cases called cysts. Sitting tight in their cysts, the eggs live on until rains dilute the water's saltiness.

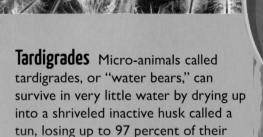

Tardigrades

Micro-animals called tardigrades, or "water bears," can survive in very little water by drying up into a shriveled inactive husk called a tun, losing up to 97 percent of their body moisture in the process.

New life in spring

Spring rain refills shrunken ponds and creates temporary pools and puddles. Triggered by moisture and longer, warmer days, the eggs that are buried in dried mud begin to hatch.

Water flea

Soon after they appear, the pools and puddles left by spring rain often teem with water fleas. This is because they can reproduce rapidly. The females do not have to wait to find a male to mate with—they reproduce asexually at first. It is only later on, when the males appear, that water fleas mate and reproduce sexually.

Molting young

All the fleas that emerge from the eggs are females. A young water flea goes through four to six molts, shedding her hard covering, or exoskeleton, and getting bigger each time. She is fully grown in less than two weeks.

Asexual eggs

The warmer weather brings a bloom of algae, the water flea's main food. The female produces asexual eggs that can hatch without being fertilized. She stores the eggs in part of her body called a brood pouch.

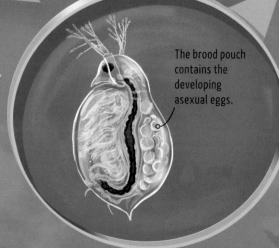

The brood pouch contains the developing asexual eggs.

Surviving winter

The egg case settles in the mud as the water evaporates. The female dies, but her resting eggs survive the cold winter in the hardened mud. They will hatch into a new generation next spring.

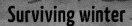

Resting eggs

The fertilized eggs are known as "resting" eggs. A hard-shelled case forms around the brood pouch inside the female. During the female's next molt, the egg case is released into the water.

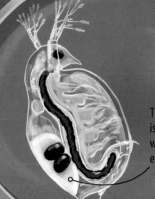

The egg case is part of the water flea's exoskeleton.

See also
Read how the water-holding frog (116–117) of Australia deals with its watery world drying up.

Fall mating

As summer turns to fall, ponds shrink, pools and puddles begin to dry up, food becomes scarce, and it becomes colder too. The female now produces sexual eggs, and she mates with the males to fertilize them.

Some female water fleas turn into males so that mating can take place.

The female "gives birth" to the babies after the eggs hatch in her brood pouch.

Summer babies

The eggs hatch in the brood pouch after about a day. The babies remain inside their mother for two or three days before she releases them into the water. Like those hatched in spring, the summer babies are all female, but a few will later change into males.

Protected eggs

After the eggs are fertilized, the female crab keeps the eggs under her body, protecting them for about 10 days until they hatch. She stirs the water with her back legs to make it flow over her eggs. Once the eggs have hatched, she leaves the hatchlings to take care of themselves.

Larvae

The eggs hatch into tiny larvae called "zoeae," which look nothing like the adult crabs. The zoeae larvae mix and drift in the ocean plankton. Many will be eaten by larger animals.

See also
Find out more about surviving in water (70–71).

Bigger larvae

Any zoeae larvae that survive develop into a larger larval stage called a megalopa.

Spider crab

The Japanese spider crab has the longest legs of any crab, at 13 ft (4 m) across. It lives in the ocean around Japan, about 650 ft (200 m) below the surface.

Coming together

The male uses his claws to transfer sperm into the female to fertilize her eggs. She produces up to 1.5 million eggs, but only a few of these will survive to become adults.

Moving to mate

In early spring, when they are ready to mate, Japanese spider crabs move from deeper water to shallower areas—about 160 ft (50 m) below the surface.

Young crab

Finally, the larvae begin to look a bit more like adult crabs. They grow in stages. Each time the crab gets too big for its shell, it wiggles out of it. It then waits for the new shell to harden up. This time is dangerous for a crab—without its hard shell it is an easy meal for a passing predator.

Tiny crabs will scavenge on detritus and graze on algae. Only the larger, more adult crabs, will have the strength to prey on animals such as hard-shelled mollusks.

Adult crab

The crab's legs will keep growing throughout its whole life. They live for more than 50 years—some scientists claim they can reach 100 years old.

Mega crabs Water helps support body weight. This means that some crabs are able to grow much bigger than they would be able to on land. The Tasmanian giant crab weighs up to 39 lb (17.6 kg).

Water babies Most crabs start off as larvae drifting in water. This means that even air-breathing land crabs such as the Christmas Island red crab must go into the water to scatter their eggs. They risk drowning while they do it.

Decorator crabs These crabs use whatever they can find around them for disguise including seaweed, coral, and sponges. Their decorations make them harder for predators to spot.

Mayfly

In summer, giant mayflies swarm over streams, rivers, and lakes in North America. Mayflies are insects that spend almost their whole lives underwater, then emerge briefly as flying adults. The adults have unworkable mouthparts, and can't feed, so they last just a short time—from minutes to days, depending on their species—during which they must find a mate.

Courtship dance

Male spinners swarm over the water, especially around sunset. They "dance" in the air, bobbing up and down to attract females. The larger females enter the swarm and mate with the males in flight.

After mating and egg laying, the spinners die. Their bodies litter the water's surface.

Egg laying

After mating, the female lays up to 8,000 fertilized eggs in the water. The eggs sink to the bottom or, thanks to their gloopy coating, stick to stones or aquatic plants.

Hatching

A giant mayfly hatches from its egg as a larva called a nymph. It sets up home in a U-shaped burrow that it makes in the mud. The nymph breathes through gills and feeds on algae and rotting material.

See also
Read about the eastern newt (114–115) that also spends part of its life underwater and part of it out of the water.

The nymph is like a flightless adult. Its developing wings are hidden under pads on its back.

The nymph spends most of its time in its burrow but occasionally comes out at night.

The spinner cannot fly until its soft new body and wings have dried and hardened.

The final stage

The dun flies off and settles on a waterside plant or tree. It is not yet ready to mate. The next day, the mayfly molts one last time and enters its last life stage—a breeding adult called a spinner.

Rising above

After one to two years living underwater, the nymph rises to the surface, where its skin splits. Out wiggles a flying adult called a dun. It rests on the water until its wings are dry.

Getting bigger

Instead of skin, the mayfly nymph has a hard covering called an exoskeleton. In order to grow, it must shed, or molt, its exoskeleton regularly—up to 30 times in all.

Mayfly blizzard Sometimes millions of mayflies invade riverside towns and villages, attracted to lights at night. They cover every available surface, and occasionally snowplows are needed to clear streets and bridges.

Great diving beetle Some aquatic insects, such as great diving beetles, continue to live in water as adults. When diving, they breathe air that they collect under their wing cases. They are able to fly off to find new ponds or slow streams to live in.

Sea skater Some insects inhabit the coast, but the only true ocean insect is the sea skater. A relative of freshwater pond skaters, the sea skater scoots over the water's surface in search of algae to feed on.

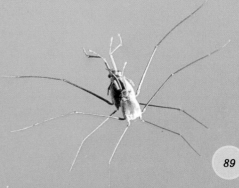

Starfish

Covered by venomous spines, the crown of thorns starfish is safe from most predators. It feeds on the corals of tropical reefs, eating the soft polyps and leaving the bare skeletons behind. Like other starfish, sea cucumbers, and sea urchins, it is a type of animal called an echinoderm.

Spawning

In summer months, the female ejects huge numbers of eggs into the water. At the same time, the male releases sperm, which swim toward the eggs and fertilize them.

Floating eggs

The fertilized eggs float among the plankton. Larvae hatch from the eggs after about a day.

A single large female produces up to 60 million eggs a year.

Drifting larvae

The larvae feed on microscopic algae called phytoplankton. The larvae are weak swimmers, so they mostly drift along with the current. Eventually, the larvae settle on the bottom.

Algal grazer

For the first six months, the baby starfish grazes at night on algae that grow on the coral reef. It moves over the reef using suckerlike tube feet on the underside of its arms.

At first, the starfish has only five stubby arms, but it soon grows more.

Attaching

Each starfish larva uses its sticky, stalklike front end to attach to a hard surface, such as rock or coral. The stalk breaks and releases the baby starfish.

Adult starfish

After two years, the starfish is much larger and ready to breed. But it will keep growing for up to two more years. It roams long distances over the reef as it searches for food.

See also
Find out about newts (114–115), which can also regrow lost limbs.

A big adult may have up to 20 arms growing out of its disk-shaped body.

The starfish pushes its stomach out of its mouth onto its prey and digests the flesh.

Coral eater

So far, the young starfish has grown slowly on its diet of algae. As it starts to feed on coral polyps, it quickly gets larger and develops a lot more arms, too.

Sea cucumber A sea cucumber has softer skin than other kinds of echinoderms. It uses its gripping tube feet to crawl over the ocean floor as it roots around for morsels of food.

Growing a new body Most starfish can grow a new arm if one has broken off. In some species, the lost arm can even turn into a whole new starfish. In the picture below, a completely new body is regrowing from the end of a discarded starfish arm.

Predators Not many predators can tackle a crown of thorns starfish—but the giant triton snail can. It injects paralyzing venom, shreds the spines with its toothed tongue, and eats the starfish.

Manatee

Too big for alligators, crocodiles, or sharks to mess with, the West Indian manatee has no natural predators, except for human hunters. This mammal is equally at home in salty coastal seas and freshwater rivers. It swims slowly with flicks of its tail and uses its flippers to "walk" over the bottom as it feeds on aquatic plants.

Grown up

After about two years with its mother, the young manatee leaves to fend for itself. In a few years, when it is more than 10 ft (3 m) long and fully grown, it will be ready to breed.

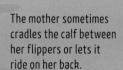

The males try to embrace her and "kiss" her back to win her approval.

Courtship

When a female manatee is ready to breed, she produces a scent to attract males. Several males flock to her and follow her around, nudging and shoving each other to try to get as close as possible.

The mother sometimes cradles the calf between her flippers or lets it ride on her back.

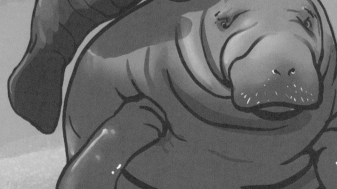

Mating and birth

The female selects one of the males, and the pair mates. She may choose to mate with other males too. After about a year, she finds a calm, sheltered place to give birth.

A calf is born

A single, dark-colored calf, about 4 ft (1.2 m) long, is born. The mother helps it to the surface to take its first breaths. Within a few hours, the calf is able to swim and surface all on its own.

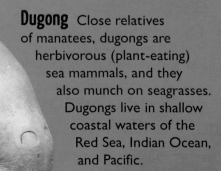

Dugong Close relatives of manatees, dugongs are herbivorous (plant-eating) sea mammals, and they also munch on seagrasses. Dugongs live in shallow coastal waters of the Red Sea, Indian Ocean, and Pacific.

Underwater meadows

Seagrasses are some of the few true plants that can grow in the sea. "Meadows" of underwater seagrasses, such as this one in Belize, provide food for marine herbivores and shelter for baby fish and other vulnerable animals.

Manatees may graze up to *7 hours* a day and *eat* more than 220 lb (100 kg) of food.

Grazing time

The manatees close off their nostrils and dive to graze on submerged plants, rising to the surface to breathe every few minutes. They strip leaves with their upper lip and grub around in sand or mud for buried stems and roots.

See also
Meet another huge underwater mammal, the northern elephant seal (96–97).

Digesting plants produces a lot of gas. By storing or releasing gas, a manatee can control its buoyancy.

Sensitive bristles on the snout help the manatee find food in murky water.

Algae often grow on the backs of manatees.

Social gatherings

Mother and calf spend most of their time on their own. Sometimes they briefly form groups with other manatees, especially where food is plentiful. There is a lot of touching and play between group members.

Early days

Like all mammal babies, the calf drinks its mother's milk. After a few weeks, it starts to nibble plants, although it continues to nurse. Touching mouths and squealing strengthens the bond between mother and calf.

The calf drinks from the teats under its mother's flipper.

Reptile visitor Green turtles, such as this one off the coast of Egypt, are regular visitors to underwater seagrass meadows. The adults are herbivores, shredding seagrasses and algae with their sawlike jaws. When young, they also eat worms, jellyfish, and crabs.

93

Orca

Although sometimes called killer whales, orcas are not actually whales at all. They are the largest type of dolphin, and one of the most powerful hunters in the ocean. They are easy to recognize by their black-and-white markings. Orca social groups are organized in a complex way, and have even developed their own dialects and cultures in different parts of the world.

Social creatures

Orcas stick together in tight family groups of less than 10, called matrilines, that are led by a dominant female. Up to three matrilines sometimes gather in bigger groups called pods. Several pods of orcas with the same dialect make up an even bigger clan.

Taking care of the young

After a 15–18 month pregnancy, the female gives birth to a single calf. She nurses her calf on milk until it is about two years old. Orcas take great care of their young, and mothers are often helped by other females in the matrilines.

Breeding

Members of a pod swim and hunt together, using their own distinctive range of sounds to communicate. At breeding time, males leave their matriline to mate with females belonging to other pods.

Walrus Walruses are found in the Arctic. They live in large groups, called herds, and lie with hundreds of other walruses on the ice. Highly social, they snort and bellow at each other. Males, however, also fight during the mating season.

See also
Read about other ocean creatures, such as the northern elephant seal (96–97) and the sand tiger shark (100–101).

Orcas lie in wait in the water to catch the seal as it is knocked off the ice.

Seal hunting

Some orcas living in Antarctica work together to catch seals on ice floes. First, they stick their heads out of the water to spot their prey. Then they swim in a group under the ice, making a huge wave that washes the seal into the water.

Orcas slap their tails on the water's surface to send messages—the sound waves made by the slap travel under the water.

Orcas in Norwegian seas catch fish by herding them into a tight ball. They slap the ball with their tails to stun or kill fish to eat. This is called "carousel feeding."

Teamwork

Orcas are among the most intelligent of all animals. They are quick learners, and can pass their knowledge on to others in the same pod. This allows family members to work together to find new and ingenious ways of catching prey.

Using sound

Orcas communicate with each other using whistles, clicks, and screams. Orcas of the same clan share the same dialect. Orcas use sound to find their way around and locate prey.

Humpback whale

A group of humpbacks is also called a pod. The whales communicate over long distances through "songs"—a series of cries, howls, and moans. Calves also "whisper" to their mothers.

Sea otter
Off the Pacific coast of North America, sea otters live in groups, called rafts. To sleep, the otters float on their backs in groups, anchoring themselves with strands of seaweed. Females also nurse their young this way.

Battle to breed

The adult males arrive on land in December, and spend a month fighting for control. Battles can last for hours, with some losers getting seriously injured. The biggest males can mate with up to 150 females, and so father the most baby seals.

New pups

When they arrive on land in January, the females are about 11 months pregnant. Their babies, or pups, are born a few days later. The females feed the pups milk for about 26 days then leave them and return to the ocean.

The pups stay on land for about two months. They only practice swimming at night, when there is less danger.

Fall arrivals

In late September, before the breeding season begins, young seals arrive on the beaches. These are juvenile seals, who are not yet ready to breed.

Elephant seal

Northern elephant seals spend most of their lives at sea, and much of their time underwater. They dive down deep into the ocean in search of food, and can hold their breath for a very long time. These seals only visit land twice a year, to breed and to shed their fur. Each trip between land and sea can be around 3,100 miles (5,000 km) long.

See also
Find out about other sea creatures that travel huge distances, such as the European eel (102–103).

Northern elephant seals mostly eat squid and fish including sharks and rays.

In a year these seals travel about 12,400 miles (20,000 km)—one of the longest migrations of any mammal.

Separate ways

When they leave their breeding beaches in California, the adult seals head off into the Pacific Ocean to feed. The males swim about 3,100 miles (5,000 km) north toward the Gulf of Alaska. The females stay south of the males, heading about 2,800 miles (4,500 km) into the central north Pacific.

Gulf of Alaska

Male range

Female range

Pacific Ocean

Male and female northern elephant seals molt at different times of the year, as do seals of different ages.

Cuvier's beaked whale
These whales can dive deeper and longer than any other mammal. Dives can last over two hours and be as deep as 9,810 ft (2,990 m) below the water's surface.

Seabirds
Some species of birds, such as albatrosses, spend most of their lives at sea, visiting land only once a year to nest.

Molting

Northern elephant seals molt their fur once a year. To do this, they swim back to the shore for about two weeks between March and July. They wait on the beach while their fur comes off in sheets.

Humpback whale
Humpback whales have one of the longest migration routes on Earth. They spend their summer breeding in warm tropical waters, and their winters feeding in polar regions. The journey can be up to 5,000 miles (8,000 km) each way.

Back to sea

Once they have molted, the seals head back out to their separate feeding grounds in the Pacific. In the ocean, they spend much of their time deep underwater. They can hold their breath for up to one hour at a time, and dive up to 5,249 ft (1,600 m) beneath the water's surface.

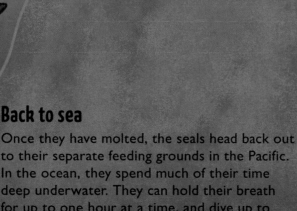

Murrelet

Few seabirds leave their nests as early as ancient murrelet chicks. These birds take to the water before they can fly—and before they have even eaten their first meal. They start their lives in nesting colonies in mossy forests on cool northern coasts, but their parents raise them entirely at sea.

Nesting time

On a spring night, after mating, a male and female pair dig a burrow. At the end of the burrow, they make a nest chamber and line it with grass, twigs, and leaves. Here, the female lays two eggs.

Burrows are dug under tree roots, logs, or clumps of grass.

Incubating the eggs

The parents take turns incubating the eggs, keeping them warm while the chicks inside develop. Each bird sits on the eggs for a few days while the other feeds at sea, then they change places.

The birds switch places at night—as one parent arrives, the other flies off.

See also
Find out how the sandgrouse takes care of its chicks by collecting water (64–65) for them to drink.

Parachuting chicks Just like ancient murrelet chicks, baby razorbills are not able to fly when they go into the water for the first time. They hurl themselves from their clifftop nests and "parachute" down into the water below.

Ready to fly Puffin chicks are fed in their nesting burrows while they grow their flight feathers. When the youngsters emerge, they fly right out to sea, ready to live on the ocean without their parents' help.

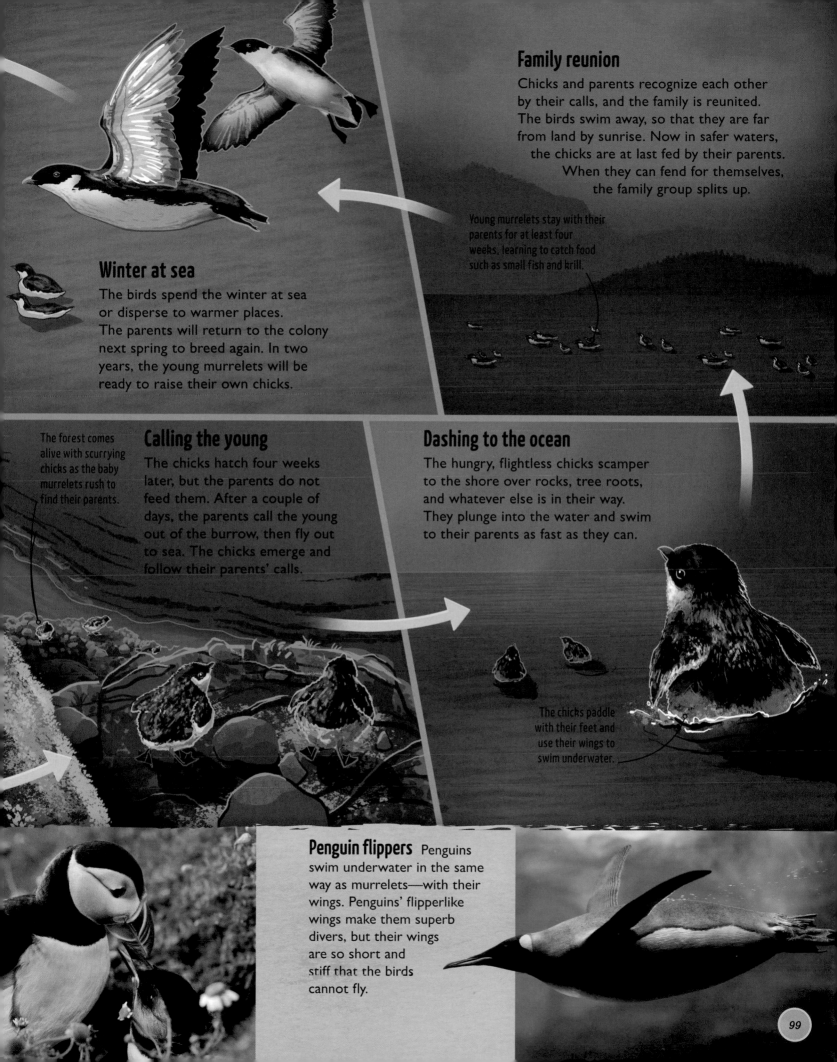

Family reunion

Chicks and parents recognize each other by their calls, and the family is reunited. The birds swim away, so that they are far from land by sunrise. Now in safer waters, the chicks are at last fed by their parents. When they can fend for themselves, the family group splits up.

Young murrelets stay with their parents for at least four weeks, learning to catch food such as small fish and krill.

Winter at sea

The birds spend the winter at sea or disperse to warmer places. The parents will return to the colony next spring to breed again. In two years, the young murrelets will be ready to raise their own chicks.

Calling the young

The chicks hatch four weeks later, but the parents do not feed them. After a couple of days, the parents call the young out of the burrow, then fly out to sea. The chicks emerge and follow their parents' calls.

The forest comes alive with scurrying chicks as the baby murrelets rush to find their parents.

Dashing to the ocean

The hungry, flightless chicks scamper to the shore over rocks, tree roots, and whatever else is in their way. They plunge into the water and swim to their parents as fast as they can.

The chicks paddle with their feet and use their wings to swim underwater.

Penguin flippers Penguins swim underwater in the same way as murrelets—with their wings. Penguins' flipperlike wings make them superb divers, but their wings are so short and stiff that the birds cannot fly.

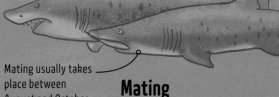

Mating usually takes place between August and October.

Mating

Sand tiger sharks often live and hunt alone, but they assemble in small groups when it's time to mate. Mating happens near the coast. Afterward, the females stay behind, while the males swim off to feed elsewhere.

Shark

A sand tiger shark lives along sandy coasts and on rocky reefs in the Atlantic, Pacific, and Indian Oceans. It shelters during the day, and hunts for other fish at night. To help it float, the shark can fill its stomach with air gulped from the water's surface. This trick lets it hover in the water, watching out for prey.

Young cannibals

The females have two uteruses where fertilized eggs hatch. After about five months, the largest, strongest baby, or pup, in each uterus eats the others. This means that only two pups survive.

When the strongest pup in each uterus grows to about 7 in (17 cm) long, it eats its siblings.

See also
Read about the deep-sea anglerfish (108–109), another sharp-toothed predator.

Great white sharks may prey on smaller sand tiger sharks.

Big babies

After a pregnancy of 8 to 12 months, the female gives birth to her two babies. The newborn pups are already about 3 ft (1 m) long. Their size helps them survive, since few predators, except other sharks, will dare to attack.

Egg cases Many shark species lay eggs instead of giving birth to live young. The eggs are protected by tough, leathery cases until they hatch. Horn sharks have spiral egg cases, which the mother shark wedges into cracks in rocks for protection.

Mermaid's purses Some egg cases are rectangular, with curly tendrils for twisting around strands of seaweed. They are known as "mermaid's purses" because of their shape.

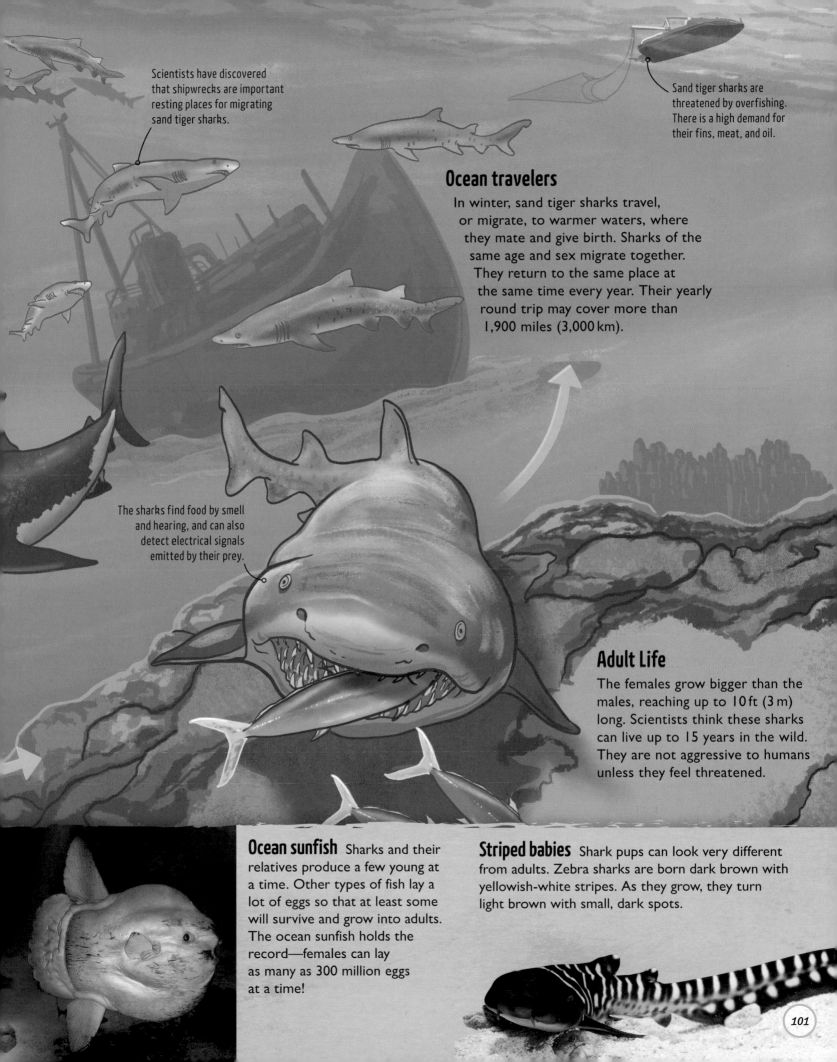

Scientists have discovered that shipwrecks are important resting places for migrating sand tiger sharks.

Sand tiger sharks are threatened by overfishing. There is a high demand for their fins, meat, and oil.

Ocean travelers

In winter, sand tiger sharks travel, or migrate, to warmer waters, where they mate and give birth. Sharks of the same age and sex migrate together. They return to the same place at the same time every year. Their yearly round trip may cover more than 1,900 miles (3,000 km).

The sharks find food by smell and hearing, and can also detect electrical signals emitted by their prey.

Adult Life

The females grow bigger than the males, reaching up to 10 ft (3 m) long. Scientists think these sharks can live up to 15 years in the wild. They are not aggressive to humans unless they feel threatened.

Ocean sunfish Sharks and their relatives produce a few young at a time. Other types of fish lay a lot of eggs so that at least some will survive and grow into adults. The ocean sunfish holds the record—females can lay as many as 300 million eggs at a time!

Striped babies Shark pups can look very different from adults. Zebra sharks are born dark brown with yellowish-white stripes. As they grow, they turn light brown with small, dark spots.

Ocean drifters

Carried by the current, the eggs drift east across the Atlantic. During this time, they hatch into larvae. It is a hazardous journey, since the eggs and larvae are food for many ocean animals.

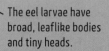

The eel larvae have broad, leaflike bodies and tiny heads.

Glass eels are about 2½ in (6 cm) long.

Journey's end

After drifting for months or even years, the larvae reach Europe. Now cylinder shaped and see-through, they are called glass eels.

Deep-sea spawning

In the spring, masses of European eels spawn deep in the ocean. They release eggs and sperm into the water and then die. The fertilized eggs float to the surface.

See also
Discover other creatures that migrate too. Read about the northern elephant seal's (96–97) journey.

Atlantic Ocean

USA

Sargasso Sea

Eel

The European eel begins and ends its life in a part of the western Atlantic Ocean called the Sargasso Sea. But in between, it spends most of its life thousands of miles away in the freshwater rivers, streams, and lakes of Europe. Its life story includes two great migrations and much change.

Zooplankton For tiny ocean animals called zooplankton, migration is a daily event. After sunset, they rise up to the surface to feed safely under the cover of darkness. To avoid surface predators, they retreat back to the depths at dawn.

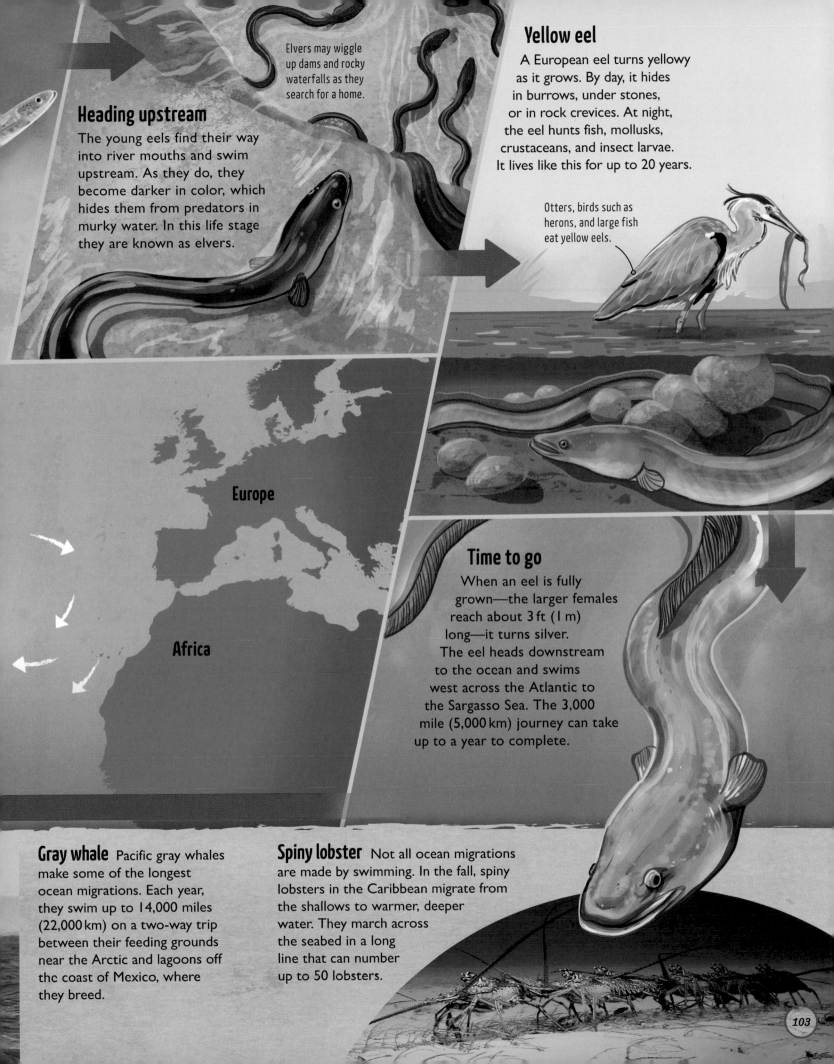

Heading upstream

The young eels find their way into river mouths and swim upstream. As they do, they become darker in color, which hides them from predators in murky water. In this life stage they are known as elvers.

Elvers may wiggle up dams and rocky waterfalls as they search for a home.

Yellow eel

A European eel turns yellowy as it grows. By day, it hides in burrows, under stones, or in rock crevices. At night, the eel hunts fish, mollusks, crustaceans, and insect larvae. It lives like this for up to 20 years.

Otters, birds such as herons, and large fish eat yellow eels.

Europe

Africa

Time to go

When an eel is fully grown—the larger females reach about 3 ft (1 m) long—it turns silver. The eel heads downstream to the ocean and swims west across the Atlantic to the Sargasso Sea. The 3,000 mile (5,000 km) journey can take up to a year to complete.

Gray whale Pacific gray whales make some of the longest ocean migrations. Each year, they swim up to 14,000 miles (22,000 km) on a two-way trip between their feeding grounds near the Arctic and lagoons off the coast of Mexico, where they breed.

Spiny lobster Not all ocean migrations are made by swimming. In the fall, spiny lobsters in the Caribbean migrate from the shallows to warmer, deeper water. They march across the seabed in a long line that can number up to 50 lobsters.

Tetra

The small South American splash tetra is unusual in being able to lay its eggs out of water—perhaps to keep them away from underwater predators. The eggs are laid on leaves hanging over the water's surface, then cared for by the male, who makes sure they don't dry out.

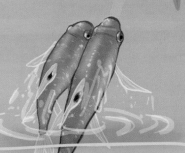

See also
Find out about how orcas (94–95) take care of their young.

The female tetra drops back to the water first, followed by the male.

The male must find a place where leaves dangle within jumping distance of the water.

Leaping from the water

Once a female has arrived, both fish leap up from the water to the underside of the leaf. The female lays about six to eight eggs, then the male fertilizes them. They stay on the leaf for a few seconds at a time, repeating the process until the female has laid up to 200 eggs.

Finding a spot

The male splash tetra looks for a spot by the bank with overhanging plant leaves. When he has found one, he displays, trying to attract a female.

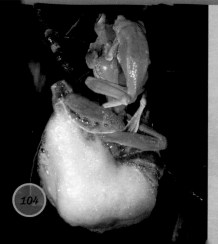

Foamy nest These tree frogs make foamy nests to keep their eggs, which hang above the water, wet. When they hatch, the tadpoles drop into a pool of water underneath the nest.

Mouth-brooding fish

Some fish, such as the male jawfish, take care of their eggs by holding them in their mouths. They cannot eat until after the eggs have hatched.

The tiny eggs must be kept wet. If they dry out, the developing fish inside will die.

The baby fish grow into adults and develop showy fins to attract mates.

Taking care of the eggs

Once the eggs have all been laid, the female swims away. The male stays near his eggs. He flips his tail fin to send water splashing up onto the eggs, to keep them wet.

Dropping to the water

After two or three days the eggs hatch. The baby fish drop down into the water below.

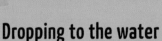

The splash tetras grow into adults in the water. They hide in leaves underwater to try to avoid being eaten.

*Splash tetras grow up to **2.7 in** (7 cm) long. They live for about **three years.***

Hatched on land Some aquatic animals start their lives on dry land before taking the plunge. Baby turtles hatch from hard-shelled eggs that are buried in an underground beach nest. After hatching, they dig themselves out before scrambling into the water.

Early days

After about a week, the eggs hatch. The larvae (babies) that emerge are all males. They float up to the surface where they spend up to two weeks growing and developing among the plankton.

The clown fish larvae become more colorful as they grow.

Guarding the eggs

The male fans the eggs with his fins. He eats any unfertilized eggs or eggs that get damaged by fungus. The female stays close by, like a sentry on guard, ready to defend the eggs against predators.

Clown fish

Small fish living on a tropical coral reef need to avoid predators on the hunt for food. Common clown fish find safety among the stinging tentacles of an anemone. The clown fish never stray far from their anemone.

The female attaches between 100 and 1,000 eggs to the rock using sticky threads.

The female tries to scare off egg thieves.

Brittle stars may attack the clown fish eggs at night.

Egg laying

A male common clown fish cleans a patch of rock beside the anemone in which he lives. He courts the female by stretching his fins, and by nibbling at her and chasing her. She lays her eggs on the patch of rock, and he fertilizes them with his sperm.

Living together
This cleaner shrimp lives in the lair of a fierce moray eel, which keeps it safe from predators. In return, the shrimp picks dead skin and parasites off the eel, and enters the eel's mouth to clean food off its jaws and teeth.

Emperor angelfish
About 500 fish species can change sex or have both male and female organs at the same time. Most, such as the emperor angelfish, change from female to male, rather than male to female like the clown fish. Young angelfish also have different color patterns compared with adults.

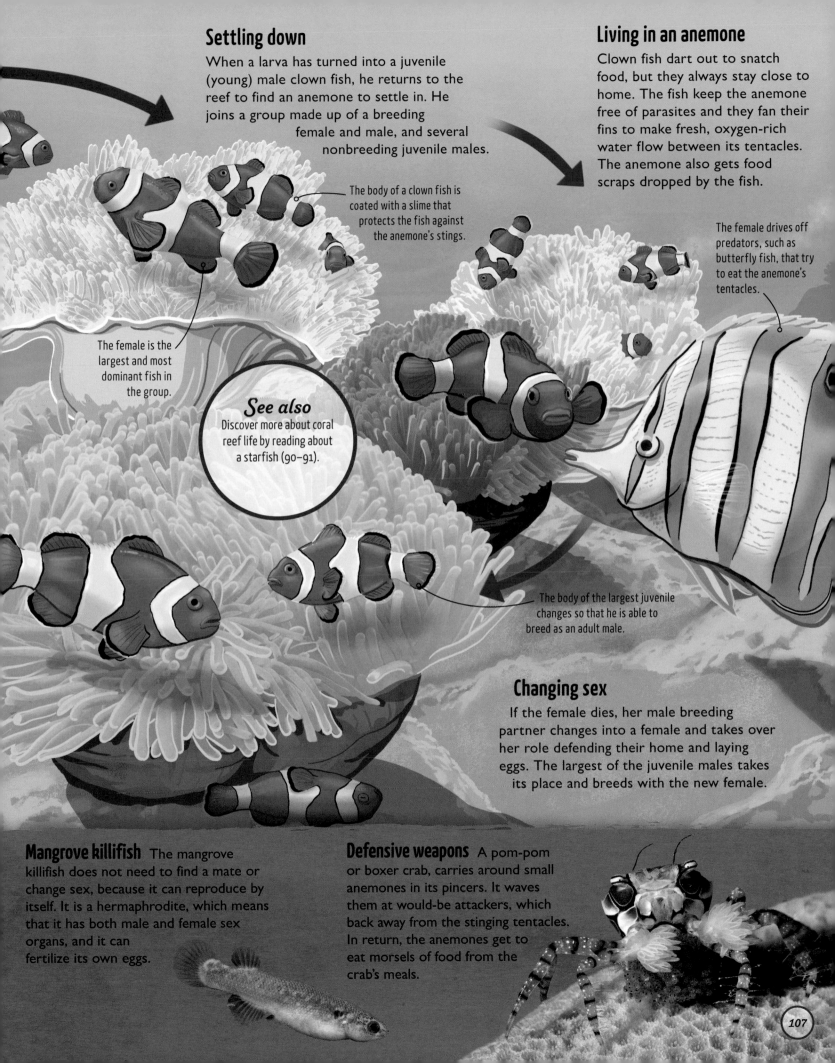

Settling down

When a larva has turned into a juvenile (young) male clown fish, he returns to the reef to find an anemone to settle in. He joins a group made up of a breeding female and male, and several nonbreeding juvenile males.

The body of a clown fish is coated with a slime that protects the fish against the anemone's stings.

Living in an anemone

Clown fish dart out to snatch food, but they always stay close to home. The fish keep the anemone free of parasites and they fan their fins to make fresh, oxygen-rich water flow between its tentacles. The anemone also gets food scraps dropped by the fish.

The female drives off predators, such as butterfly fish, that try to eat the anemone's tentacles.

The female is the largest and most dominant fish in the group.

See also
Discover more about coral reef life by reading about a starfish (90–91).

The body of the largest juvenile changes so that he is able to breed as an adult male.

Changing sex

If the female dies, her male breeding partner changes into a female and takes over her role defending their home and laying eggs. The largest of the juvenile males takes its place and breeds with the new female.

Mangrove killifish The mangrove killifish does not need to find a mate or change sex, because it can reproduce by itself. It is a hermaphrodite, which means that it has both male and female sex organs, and it can fertilize its own eggs.

Defensive weapons A pom-pom or boxer crab, carries around small anemones in its pincers. It waves them at would-be attackers, which back away from the stinging tentacles. In return, the anemones get to eat morsels of food from the crab's meals.

Anglerfish

Finding food is a challenge for animals of the deep, dark ocean. To solve the problem, the humpback anglerfish goes fishing for its dinner by waving a glowing "lantern." Curious prey approach, lured by the light, only to be snatched by the anglerfish's massive, sharp-toothed jaws.

Fish fry

Humpback anglerfish eggs hatch at the ocean's surface. The young anglerfish, called fry, feed on tiny plankton as they grow. When the fry are large enough, they swim down into the gloomy depths.

Slow-swimming predator

In the deep, murky, icy water, humpback anglerfish live alone. They swim too slowly and awkwardly to chase prey. Instead, they ambush other fish that wander close enough for them to grab.

The fish swims along with a wobbly wiggle, and jaws gaping wide.

The flashing "lantern" sits on a long spine, which the anglerfish moves back and forth.

Fishing lure

Only females have a flashing "lantern" to attract prey. Millions of light-producing bacteria set up home in the lantern. In return for making the lantern glow, the anglerfish supplies them with nutrients.

Connected forever

When some deep-sea anglerfish species mate, the male never lets go of the female. His body fuses (joins) with hers. Her body provides him with nourishment, and he is always there to fertilize her eggs.

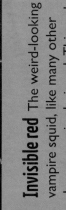

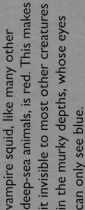

Invisible red The weird-looking vampire squid, like many other deep-sea animals, is red. This makes it invisible to most other creatures in the murky depths, whose eyes can only see blue.

Shrimp defense

Some deep-ocean animals use flashes or bursts of light to defend themselves. There are even shrimp that squirt a glowing blue fluid into the water to startle predators. This gives the shrimp time to escape.

Glowing ocean

Just like the bacteria in the anglerfish's lantern, some tiny algae called phytoplankton can also use chemicals to create light. They make the ocean sparkle like a starry sky.

See also

Discover more about how animals survive at different depths in the ocean (72–73).

Big mouth, big meals

Because food is scarce, the female anglerfish's meals need to be as big as possible. Her lower jaw opens wide enough to swallow victims whole, and her stomach stretches to hold large prey.

Toothy grip

Using his teeth, the male clamps on tightly to the female's body. As she lays her eggs into the water, he releases sperm to fertilize them. The eggs float up to the surface.

After mating, the male swims off in search of other females.

The male's large eyes and nostrils help him find a mate.

Waiting for a mate

The female must wait for a mate to find her in the dark. The small male has a superb sense of smell that allows him to pick up and follow her scent. Eventually, he spots her glowing lure.

Ichthyosaur

Ichthyosaurs were marine reptiles that appeared around the start of the Mesozoic era (252 million years ago). There were many species, ranging in length from about 3.3 ft (1 m) to 66 ft (20 m). Larger species were the top predators in their marine habitats. Ichthyosaurs died out about 90 million years ago, for unknown reasons.

Pregnancy

Little is known about how ichthyosaurs mated, though we have many fossils of pregnant females. From these fossils, we can see that ichthyosaurs didn't lay eggs. The unborn babies developed inside their mother.

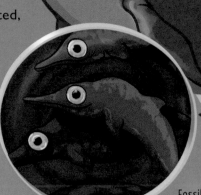

Fossils of pregnant ichthyosaurs contain between 1 and 11 unborn babies,

Live birth

It is thought that ichthyosaurs usually gave birth tail first to help reduce the chance of the newborn drowning before it eventually broke away from its mother. But, just like modern whales and dolphins, head-first births sometimes happened too.

Growing up

These predators grew quickly. Young ichthyosaurs probably stayed in shallow water, where it was safe. When big enough, they swam out to the deep, open ocean.

Squidlike belemnites and spiral-shelled ammonites were the favorite food of many ichthyosaur species.

Venturing deeper

Adult ichthyosaurs most likely hunted by using their excellent eyesight to spot prey. Some species had exceptionally large eyes, which may have allowed them to venture deep into dark waters to find food.

Keeping warm

Ichthyosaurs were well suited to life in the ocean. There is evidence that they had a layer of fat, or blubber, under the skin. This probably means that they were warm-blooded— able to keep a constantly high body temperature in the water.

Although they look like fish, ichthyosaurs were reptiles, and had to rise to the water's surface to breathe air.

Ichthyosaurs evolved from egg-laying, land-living reptiles.

Scientists have found skin pigment cells in some ichthyosaur fossils. This gives them an idea of the reptiles' natural coloring.

Countershading

Some ichthyosaurs may have had dark backs and light bellies—a type of camouflage called countershading. Many marine animals are colored this way to remain unseen by predators and prey. It helps them blend in with the ocean depths when viewed from above, and the bright sky when viewed from below.

See also

Read about the sea snake (112–113), another marine reptile that gives birth to live young in the ocean.

Marine reptiles

The Mesozoic oceans were full of other marine reptiles, including long-necked plesiosaurs (above), gigantic pliosaurs, and ferocious mosasaurs.

Seafood diet

The cephalopods, such as belemnites and ammonites, that ichthyosaurs preyed on are related to today's cephalopods, including squid, octopuses, and cuttlefish (below).

Dolphin shaped

Ichthyosaurs looked like modern dolphins. The process in which unrelated species living in a similar environment develop the same features is called convergent evolution.

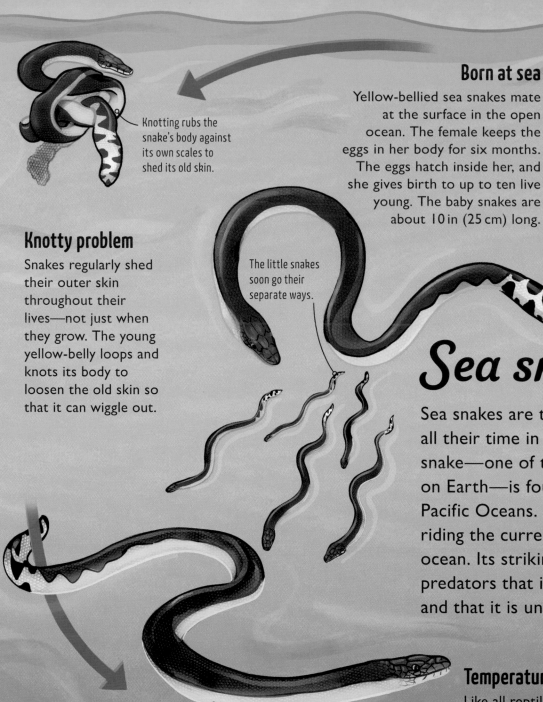

Knotty problem

Snakes regularly shed their outer skin throughout their lives—not just when they grow. The young yellow-belly loops and knots its body to loosen the old skin so that it can wiggle out.

Knotting rubs the snake's body against its own scales to shed its old skin.

Born at sea

Yellow-bellied sea snakes mate at the surface in the open ocean. The female keeps the eggs in her body for six months. The eggs hatch inside her, and she gives birth to up to ten live young. The baby snakes are about 10 in (25 cm) long.

The little snakes soon go their separate ways.

Sea snake

Sea snakes are the only reptiles that spend all their time in water. The yellow-bellied sea snake—one of the most widespread snakes on Earth—is found throughout the Indian and Pacific Oceans. It lives completely out at sea, riding the currents back and forth across the ocean. Its striking colors warn would-be predators that it has a powerful venom, and that it is unpleasant to eat.

The snake has lungs, not gills, but during dives it can absorb oxygen from the water through its skin.

Temperature control

Like all reptiles, the yellow-belly is cold-blooded, meaning that its body temperature depends on its surroundings. If the young snake needs to warm up, it basks in the sun at the surface. When it gets too warm, it dives deeper to cool off.

Saltwater crocodile

The saltwater crocodile, the world's largest reptile, lives in rivers, estuaries, along coasts, and in the open ocean. The "salty" is a powerful swimmer, and it has been spotted in the ocean 600 miles (1,000 km) from land.

Egg-laying sea snake

Though yellow-bellies and other true sea snakes may get washed up on beaches, they never deliberately go onto land. But sea kraits, which also live in the ocean, come ashore to lay their eggs, shed their skin, and digest their prey.

The snake swims by sending waves of side-to-side movement along its body, helped by its wide, paddlelike tail.

Waiting for rain

The juvenile snake can't drink saltwater—it only drinks freshwater that builds up on the surface of the ocean during heavy rain. If it doesn't rain, the snake goes thirsty.

Ocean wanderer

Now fully grown, the snake is about 3 ft (1 m) long. It can swim both forward and backward—and quickly if it needs to—but it mostly drifts with the current. During its two to three years of life, it can travel many thousands of miles.

Slick snakes

Long lines of floating seaweed, foam, and debris may build up in the slicks, washed together by the converging currents. Large numbers of yellow-bellies gather here, along with fish, plankton, and other marine life.

The snake paralyzes the fish with its venom, then swallows it whole.

Ambush predator

The growing snake drifts motionless in lanes of calm water, called "slicks," that form where ocean currents meet. Fish that swim close by, or that make the mistake of sheltering below it, are snatched with a lightning-fast lunge.

See also
Read about a prehistoric ocean reptile called an ichthyosaur (110–111).

Marine iguana The marine iguana is the only lizard that forages for food in the ocean. It dives down as far as 39 ft (12 m) to nibble seaweed, staying submerged for up to an hour. When not feeding in the cold water, the iguana suns itself on rocky shores.

Newt

Like frogs and other amphibians, newts live a double life—part of it in water, and part of it on land. Moving between the two habitats, their bodies go through great changes to adjust to the different conditions. The Eastern newt of North America lives in ponds, marshes, and small lakes, but it also spends time in the woods among the leaf litter.

The adult's tail has become broader and flatter for swimming.

Back to water

Now an adult, the newt returns to the water. It spends the rest of its life in a pond or other wet habitats. It still has lungs, so it must come up to the surface to breathe.

Courting couple

A male adult newt courts a female by performing a "dance" and then embracing her. If she accepts him, he lays a package of sperm on the muddy floor. The female takes the package into her body, where the sperm fertilize her eggs.

The adult is no longer bright red—its skin is still poisonous, but not as toxic as when it was an eft.

Laying eggs on water plants shelters the eggs and keeps them hidden from predators.

The male grips the female and wafts his scent toward her nose with his tail.

Laying eggs

The female lays one egg at a time on an underwater leaf or stem. She may wrap part of the plant around the egg to hide it. She lays a few eggs every day for a few weeks.

Sperm package

See also
The mayfly (88–89) also spends its early life in the water before leaving to develop outside of water.

The eft's red skin warns predators that it is poisonous to eat.

Land-living eft

After two to three months, the tadpole grows lungs and loses its gills. It is now a land-living juvenile called an eft. This change is called metamorphosis. The eft lives on land for up to seven years, eating small creatures it finds in the soil or under leaves.

The feathery gills are just behind the tadpole's head.

Underwater living

The tadpole has gills for breathing in water and a tail for swimming, and it gradually grows legs. It is a hungry hunter that catches small animals such as water fleas, snails, and the larvae of beetles and mosquitoes.

Newts can grow a new leg if they lose one.

The tadpole's skin contains poison that wards off many predators.

The baby grows inside the egg for two to three weeks.

Hatching

The mother newt leaves the eggs to develop and hatch on their own. When the baby newt, or tadpole, emerges from the egg, it feeds on the remains of the yolk for a few days.

Treetop tadpoles

Bromeliads are plants that grow high up on rainforest trees. Some tropical frogs lay their eggs in the tiny pools of rainwater that collect in the center of the plants. The tadpoles eat algae and insect larvae that they find in the water.

Amphibians that mate

Caecilians are legless, wormlike amphibians. Caecilian eggs are fertilized inside the female. Unlike newts, they don't do this with a sperm package. Instead, the male and female caecilians mate and he transfers sperm directly into her body.

Spawning embrace

Most frogs fertilize their eggs in water. When the adults spawn, males cling tightly to females so that they release their sperm and eggs close together. This makes it more likely that the eggs will be fertilized.

Frog

The amazing water-holding frog lives in southern Australia—in swamps, creeks, and grasslands. Very little rain falls here, but the water-holding frog has an extraordinary way of dealing with changing weather conditions.

While buried, the adult frog lives off fat stored in its body.

Digging deep

At dry times of the year, the water on the surface dries up. Using its feet as spades, the water-holding frog burrows deep into the sandy ground. It can dig up to 3 ft (1 m) down.

Burrowing

The young frog starts to dig its burrow in the ground. It will stay there until the next rainfall comes—then the cycle will begin again.

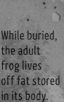

See also
Find out about other amphibians, which live on land and in the water, such as the Eastern newt (114–115).

Changeover

It takes the tadpoles about 30 days to turn into adult frogs that can live on land. The young frog must get back underground before the sandy ground is too hard to dig.

The tadpoles grow quickly, reaching up to 2.3 in (60 mm) in length.

Kangaroo rats Kangaroo rats live in western North America. They never have to drink because they get all the water they need from the seeds they eat. They also make very strong, concentrated urine, which helps cut down the amount of water they lose.

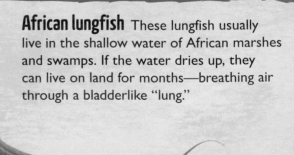

African lungfish These lungfish usually live in the shallow water of African marshes and swamps. If the water dries up, they can live on land for months—breathing air through a bladderlike "lung."

Keeping moist

The frog lines its burrow with a layer of skin and slimy mucus. This waterproof layer hardens like a bag around the frog's body. It helps keep water in, and stops the frog from drying out.

Waking up

When rain comes, water soaks into the frog's burrow. This is the signal for the frog to wake up. It crawls out from its bag, which it then eats for nourishment.

The frog also stores water in its bladder and under its skin—enough to double its weight.

The water-holding frog can live up to five years without drinking!

Laying eggs

After mating, the female lays many of her eggs in the water—up to 500 at a time. The clumps of frog spawn cling to plants in the water or float on the surface. A few weeks later, the eggs hatch into large, golden-green tadpoles.

Special call

Males must find a mate quickly before the water dries up again. They gather at the edge of small pools of water, and call loudly to females "maaw-w-w, maaw-w-w."

Desert tortoise

In hot, dry weather, desert tortoises store water in their bladder. These desert tortoises live in Mexico and the US. When it rains, they fill their bladder with water, and then in the dry season, they extract water through their bladder walls.

Waxy monkey tree frog

These tree frogs live in the dry Chaco region of South America. They secrete a waxy substance from special glands in their skin which they wipe over the surface of their body using their arms and legs. This substance prevents water loss.

Zooxanthellae
(zoh~uh~zan~thel~ee)

The spectacular life and colors of a tropical coral reef rely on an amazing partnership between the tiny coral polyps that build the reef and the single-celled algae that live inside them. The algae, called zooxanthellae, get a safe home. In return, they supply the coral with much of the food it needs.

Free swimming

The algae spend part of their life cycle swimming freely as part of the plankton. Like plants, they use sunlight to make their own sugary food by photosynthesis.

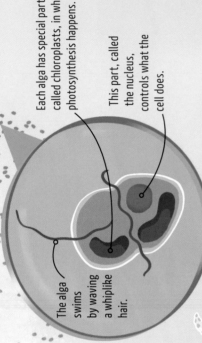

Each alga has special parts called chloroplasts, in which photosynthesis happens.

This part, called the nucleus, controls what the cell does.

The alga swims by waving a whiplike hair.

Swallowed up

A flowerlike coral polyp on the reef swallows the algae as it takes in water through its mouth. Cells in the polyp's body "capture" the algae, which then lose their whiplike hairs.

The polyp's see-through flesh allows sunlight to reach the algae.

Back into the plankton

The polyp gets rid of the algae that have swimming hairs. These join other microscopic algae and animals in the plankton. The polyp keeps any algae that don't have swimming hairs, and these continue to help make food.

Partnership

Inside the polyp, the algae use carbon dioxide produced by the polyp to make their food by photosynthesis. Some of this food passes back to the polyp to supplement what it gets by catching prey with its tentacles.

Corals live together as colonies of many tiny polyps joined together. Over time, their hard, chalky skeletons build up to form enormous coral reefs.

Corals thrive in shallow waters bathed in sunlight, providing fuel for their zooxanthellae.

The algae live in the polyp's flesh.

Making more algae

While living in the polyp, each zooxanthella reproduces by dividing in two. Both the new cells are copies of the "mother" cell. Some of the new algae have swimming hairs, and some do not.

Each new cell divides in two.

See also

Find out about how photosynthesis works (56–57).

Coral colors Corals get many of their beautiful colors from the pigment chemicals that their zooxanthellae use to trap the sun's energy. The pigment chlorophyll makes green and brownish colors.

Underwater sunscreen Some corals can make their own pink or purple pigments. These colors shield the algae in the corals from harmful rays in sunlight that might damage them, like the way sunscreen protects human skin.

Bleached coral When the water becomes too warm or polluted, corals eject their algae, leaving it white or "bleached." If the water conditions do not improve, the coral will die. Rising ocean temperatures due to global warming are causing coral bleaching worldwide.

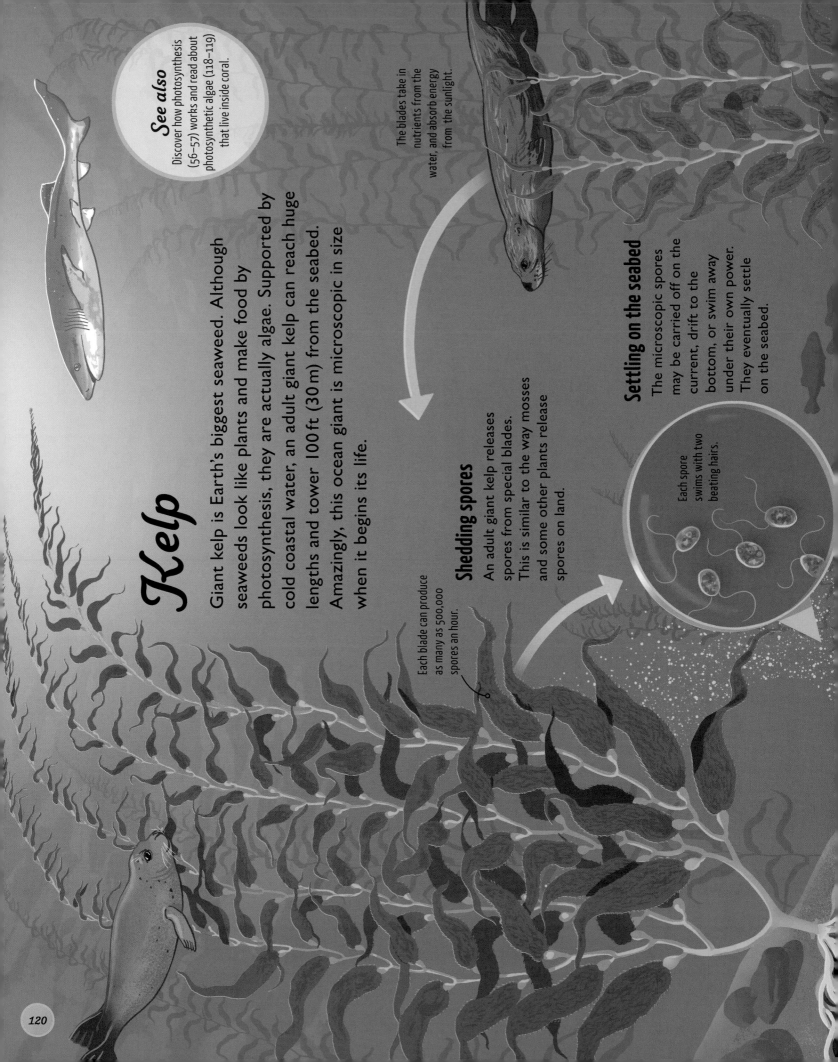

See also

Discover how photosynthesis (56–57) works and read about photosynthetic algae (118–119) that live inside coral.

The blades take in nutrients from the water, and absorb energy from the sunlight.

Kelp

Giant kelp is Earth's biggest seaweed. Although seaweeds look like plants and make food by photosynthesis, they are actually algae. Supported by cold coastal water, an adult giant kelp can reach huge lengths and tower 100ft (30m) from the seabed. Amazingly, this ocean giant is microscopic in size when it begins its life.

Shedding spores

An adult giant kelp releases spores from special blades. This is similar to the way mosses and some other plants release spores on land.

Each blade can produce as many as 500,000 spores an hour.

Settling on the seabed

The microscopic spores may be carried off on the current, drift to the bottom, or swim away under their own power. They eventually settle on the seabed.

Each spore swims with two beating hairs.

Making food

Like plant leaves, the blades of the frond absorb energy from sunlight and use it to make sugary food for the giant kelp by photosynthesis. The older the kelp gets, the more fronds it grows. Some giant kelps have hundreds of fronds.

First frond

Secured by the holdfast, the young kelp can safely develop. It grows a frond made up of a stem, called a stipe, that supports leaflike blades. At the base of each blade is a gas-filled "balloon" that acts as a float.

Sprouting

The spores sprout. Still microscopic, they now look like tiny balls of blue or gold fluff. The blue balls release swimming sperm, which fertilize eggs attached to the golden balls.

Female forms produce eggs.

Male forms produce sperm.

Each fertilized egg begins to develop into a baby giant kelp.

Holding on

The young kelp that grows from a fertilized egg sends out little tendrils that wrap around and attach to rocks, stones, or other material on the seabed. Together, these tendrils make up the holdfast, which anchors the kelp firmly to the bottom.

The holdfast stops the kelp from being carried away by the current.

Ocean haven "Forests" of giant kelp, with their spreading fronds, provide shelter for fish and other ocean animals, while invertebrates such as sea urchins and snails graze on the holdfasts. Seals and sea lions weave through the forests as they hunt for fish.

Phytoplankton Most algae stay microscopic for their entire lives. Called phytoplankton, they provide food for many aquatic animals.

Seaweed colors Like plants, seaweeds use the green pigment chlorophyll to capture the energy of sunlight. But not all seaweeds are green. To trap underwater light better, some seaweeds have other light-absorbing pigments, making them red or, like giant kelp, brown.

Water and humans

Water is a vital part of our everyday lives. We rely on it to prepare our food, to wash ourselves, and to clean our clothes. A network of pipes ensures that we can send water to wherever it is needed. Water is also used to grow crops, to transport goods, and to generate electricity. Water is precious and versatile—let's not waste it!

Depending on *water*

People rely on water. It is vital for growing crops and raising farm animals. Oceans and seas, rivers and lakes are rich sources of food. People travel, trade, and explore on water.

All crops need regular watering to grow well. It can take about 660 gallons (2,500 l) of water to produce $2\frac{1}{5}$ lb (1 kg) of rice.

A replica of HMS *Endeavour*, the first ship from Europe to reach eastern Australia in 1770, captained by English explorer James Cook.

Food source

Water is home to an incredible range of living things. This includes millions of tons of seaweed, fish, shrimp, and other living things that people eat. About 17 percent of all the protein people eat comes from the planet's oceans. In some coastal countries, that figure rises to 50 percent.

Travel and exploration

Before cars, trains, and airplanes, people explored and traveled long distances by ship. Explorers, such as Zheng He from China and Christopher Columbus and Vasco da Gama from Europe, found new sea routes, opening up travel and trade.

More than 170 million tons of fish and other seafood, such as shrimp, are raised or caught each year.

Fresh vegetables and fruit may need to be rinsed to remove bugs, dirt, and traces of chemicals used to help them grow.

Preparing food

Water is essential for cleaning, preparing, and cooking food for meals. It is used for boiling and steaming foods, and for preparing sauces, batter, and dough. Water is also needed to clean pans, plates, and utensils after the food has been eaten.

About 90 percent of everything you buy has traveled by ship at some point.

Container ships carry a variety of cargo. Each container can hold a surprisingly large amount of items, such as 12,000 shoeboxes, or more than 40,000 bananas!

Trade and shipping

Today, billions of tons of goods and raw materials crisscross the globe on water—carried by container ships, tankers, and other vessels. Some giant cargo ships can carry more than 7,000 cars or 20,000 containers at a time. Large ports on the coast handle thousands of ships a year.

On the coast

Most of the world's major cities were founded close to water so that they could trade. Eight out of the ten largest cities are located on the coast or on river mouths close to the ocean. Many other cities are positioned beside a major river, giving them access to the ocean and other cities.

Shanghai in China is the world's busiest port.

Hydropower

The movement of water can be used to make power—this is called hydropower. One way this is done is by building huge dams across rivers. As the river water flows down through the dam, it turns the blades of a device called a turbine. The turbine then spins a generator, producing electricity.

Tide power

Ocean tides move up and down our shores twice a day. Tidal power plants use this movement to turn turbines or paddles, creating electricity.

*The oldest dam still in use is the **Lake Homs Dam** in Syria. It was built during the reign of the Egyptian Pharoah Sethi, more than **3,000 years** ago.*

Penstock

Reservoir

Building the dam Dams are built across large rivers, in places where there is a steep drop, so that water will have a long way to travel from the top of the dam down to the river below.

Open the gates! To create power, the intake gates on the dam are opened. This lets water flow out of the reservoir where it is held. The water moves downward, through a pipe called the penstock.

Screw turbine

Smaller rivers can also be used to make electricity, using screw turbines. The water flows into the screw at the top, and the weight of the water makes the screw turn, powering a generator.

Fish ladder

Salmon travel up rivers every year to lay their eggs. Building dams on their rivers blocks them from doing this. Some dams now have "fish ladders" to let the salmon get past.

Three Gorges Dam

The biggest dam in the world is the Three Gorges Dam in China. Completed in 2006, it is 1.4 miles (2.3 km) wide and 630 ft (192 m) high.

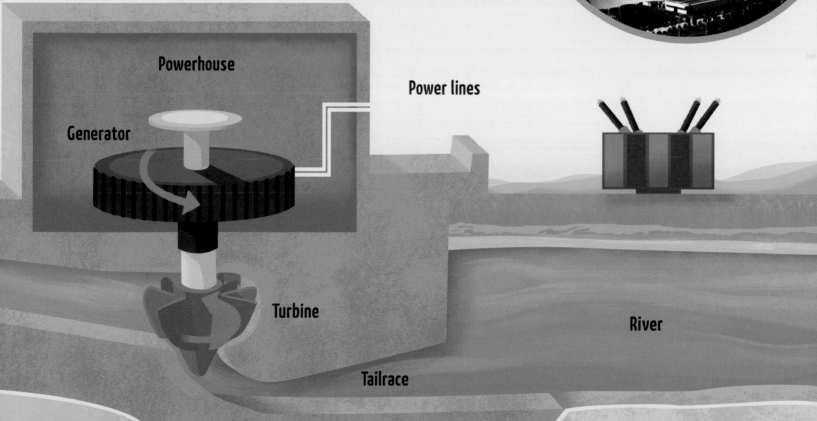

Powerhouse

Power lines

Generator

River

Turbine

Tailrace

Making power At the end of the penstock the flow of water hits the blades of a turbine, making them turn. The shaft of the turbine goes up into the generator, which spins, producing electricity. Power lines carry the electricity away from the dam.

Water moves on The used water keeps flowing past the turbine, through a pipe called a tailrace, and back into the river. The water is moving very fast when it emerges.

Irrigation

In many places farmers cannot rely on enough regular rainfall to guarantee their crops will do well. So, they must find ways of watering their plants artificially. This process is called irrigation and was first practiced in Asia and the Middle East more than 6,000 years ago. Today, farmers use different types of irrigation systems to make sure they get good harvests.

Water storage

At some farms, wells are dug to access water that lies deep underground. In other places, water is stored in artificial reservoirs or large tanks.

Overhead sprinklers

Water is pumped along pipes that connect to sprinklers. These spray fine droplets onto the crops below. The sprinklers can be set in one place or be on a wheeled frame that moves through a field.

Filtered and pumped

Water travels from the well to the top of a filter tank. It is filtered by passing it through sand which traps dirt and algae. The cleaned water is then pumped into the pipes of the irrigation system.

Drip by drip

Drip irrigation has networks of narrow pipes that run in rows. Each pipe has tiny holes, or nozzles, through which water flows directly to the roots of each plant. It wastes less water than other systems.

Surface irrigation

Simple irrigation can occur on the surface of sloping fields. Furrows are long, shallow channels dug between rows of crops. The force of gravity makes water flow down the furrows reaching all the crops in the field.

Eyes in the sky

Drones fly above farms and use cameras and sensors to measure how dry and warm certain fields are. Some can even deliver an instant watering.

A pattern of circular crop fields dot the landscape of Colorado, US.

70 *percent of all the* **freshwater** *used around the world goes toward growing* **crops** *and raising farm animals.*

Central pivot irrigation

These large overhead sprinklers are turned by an electric motor at one end. The other end sweeps around while the sprinklers spray in a large circle. It can take 12–21 hours for a large, circular field to be watered.

A field using central pivot irrigation can be about 2870–3280 ft (800–1,000 m) in diameter.

Water in the home

Every day, you rely on water at home, not just to drink but to wash, cook, and clean with. A network of water pipes runs around your home delivering water to where it is needed—from the faucets of a kitchen sink to toilets and showers. A second network of pipes carries wastewater away.

Plumbed in

A kitchen sink has hot and cold water supplied via pipes. Some household appliances, such as dishwashers, may be plumbed into the water supply with their very own pipes. A refrigerator-freezer may only require a cold-water pipe to supply its ice maker. A washing machine may have both hot- and cold- water pipes.

A pipe may run to an outside faucet for cleaning and watering lawns and gardens.

Cold water flows through a series of snaking pipes inside a boiler where it absorbs heat.

Water supply

Clean, fresh water travels underground, through the town or city water pipes. Water-supply lines carry water from these pipes to individual homes. The pipes often have a shut-off valve, which can be closed to cut off the water supply. In some houses, the water flows past a water meter which measures how much is used.

Heating up

Hot water, made by a boiler or water heater, travels to faucets and showerheads. Some may be diverted to a separate network of pipes. These let hot water flow through radiators in rooms to warm the surrounding air and provide heating.

A high~pressure shower can use 4 gallons (15 liters) of water every minute.

Off for treatment

Sewage pipes carry the water to a sewage treatment plant. Here, the water is filtered and cleaned thoroughly before it is returned to the water supply.

A soil pipe carries waste away from a toilet when it is flushed.

See also
Discover how water is used in irrigation (128–129) to grow our food.

Drained away

A system of waste pipes carries dirty, or wastewater, away that flows down sink and bath drains. The wastewater runs out of the house and flows into the public sewage pipes.

Wasted water
More than 800 million people lack access to clean water. In contrast, homes in other parts of the world often waste a lot of water. A single leaking faucet can lead to more than 1,320 gallons (5,000 liters) of clean water going to waste in one year.

Saving water
A running faucet uses 1.3–5.2 gallons (5–20 liters) of water every minute. Turning the faucet off while brushing your teeth, and using watering cans rather than hoses outside, are easy ways to save water.

Rainwater collection
Many homes can reduce their city water use by collecting rainwater that runs off roofs, and storing it in rain barrels. This water can be used outside, or if extra plumbing is installed, to flush toilets.

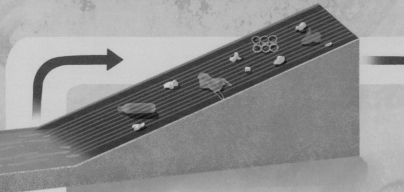

Screening

When the dirty water reaches the treatment plant, it goes through several stages of cleaning. First, it is sent through a grid to remove any trash, such as cans, plastic bags, and diapers. This is called screening.

Removing dirt

Next, the water is pumped into big, deep containers called sedimentation tanks. Heavy pieces of waste, such as poop, sink to the bottom of the tank, making a layer of sludge. The sludge is taken away. It is made into fertilizer or burned to release energy.

Sludge

Wastewater

The water flows through pipes, which connect with a network of sewers. The sewer system carries the dirty water, or wastewater, to the treatment plant where it gets cleaned.

See also
Find out more about how we use water in the home (130–131).

Flushing the toilet sends its contents down a pipe that connects to a bigger pipe, called a sewer.

Wastewater

We use water every day. But have you ever wondered where it goes when we're finished with it? A series of pipes, called a sewer system, takes dirty water away from our homes and other buildings. This wastewater is taken to a treatment plant, where it is cleaned before being returned to rivers or the ocean.

Treating sludge The sludge that is removed from sewer water has to be treated but can then be used to feed plants. It is sent into large tanks called digesters, where it is broken down by bacteria. Then it is dried into granules that farmers can spread on their fields.

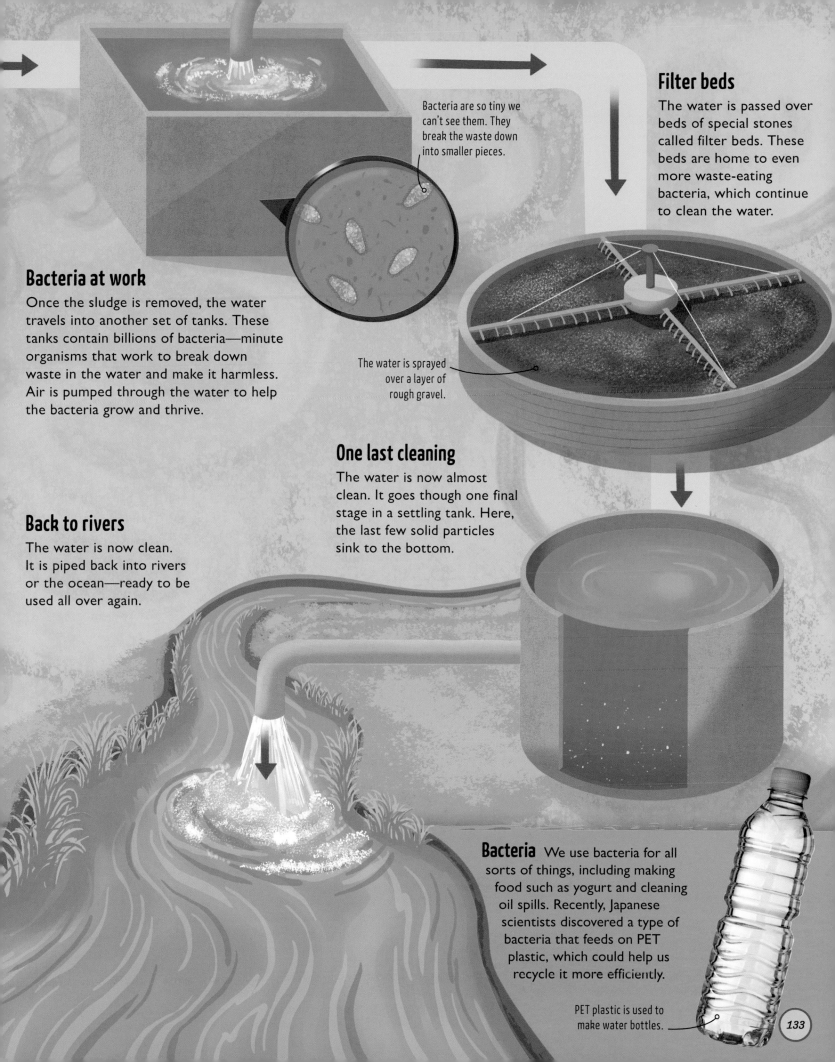

Bacteria are so tiny we can't see them. They break the waste down into smaller pieces.

Filter beds

The water is passed over beds of special stones called filter beds. These beds are home to even more waste-eating bacteria, which continue to clean the water.

Bacteria at work

Once the sludge is removed, the water travels into another set of tanks. These tanks contain billions of bacteria—minute organisms that work to break down waste in the water and make it harmless. Air is pumped through the water to help the bacteria grow and thrive.

The water is sprayed over a layer of rough gravel.

One last cleaning

The water is now almost clean. It goes though one final stage in a settling tank. Here, the last few solid particles sink to the bottom.

Back to rivers

The water is now clean. It is piped back into rivers or the ocean—ready to be used all over again.

Bacteria We use bacteria for all sorts of things, including making food such as yogurt and cleaning oil spills. Recently, Japanese scientists discovered a type of bacteria that feeds on PET plastic, which could help us recycle it more efficiently.

PET plastic is used to make water bottles.

133

Water in a skyscaper

Towering skyscrapers are found in many cities of the world. Rising 2,716 ft (828 m) above the ground, the Burj Khalifa in Dubai is the tallest of them all. Almost twice as high as the Empire State Building in the US, it contains 160 floors where people live and work. It can hold up to 10,000 people, and vast amounts of water have to be carried to all parts of this giant building.

On average, the Burj Khalifa uses 250,000 gallons (946,000 liters) of water a day—enough water to fill more than 6,000 baths.

Pipe network

More than 132 miles (212 km) of pipes make up the building's fire emergency system, with 43,000 water sprinklers. There are also 21 miles (33.6 km) of pipes carrying chilled water to keep rooms cool. Both systems run on separate pumps and controls from the regular water supply.

Drainage pipes running down from toilets and sinks are soundproofed so that people don't hear the falling water.

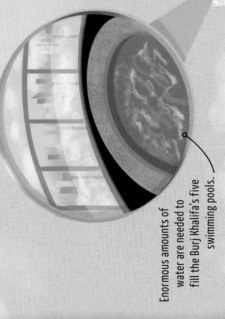

Enormous amounts of water are needed to fill the Burj Khalifa's five swimming pools.

Pressure zone

The water in a break tank supplies a certain pressure zone of the building—a number of floors immediately above and below the tank. Extra booster pumps on the mechanical floor are used to push the water higher up to the next break tank.

Collecting condensation

Air inside the Burj Khalifa is cooler than the hot, humid weather outside. This causes water vapor in the air to condense on the building's glass. About 18 million gallons (68 million liters) of condensation is created each year. Most of this is collected by a system of pipes that fill a large tank in the building's underground parking garage. This water supplies fountains and waters the gardens that surround the skyscraper.

Break tank

Break tanks

Water is pumped up the building in stages. Each stage has a giant water-storage tank called a break tank. The Burj Khalifa has four of these tanks on the 73–75th, 109–111th, 136–138th, and 155–156th floors. They each hold 237,755 gallons (900,000 liters).

Pump it up

The city's water supply has enough pressure to force water up a short distance. The building's series of powerful pumps must do the rest. These pumps are highly pressurized—with about 30 times the pressure of the atmosphere pressing down on Earth.

Tanks on the roof

When the first high-rise city buildings were built, engineers added large tanks on top of the roofs. Motorized pumps pushed the water from the ground level up through the building to fill each tank. Water then flowed back down through supply pipes whenever it was needed. The pumps could be switched back on for short periods, pumping more water to keep the roof tank full.

Some 70 miles (113 km) of supply pipes carry water from the break tanks to each part of the building.

Coming down

Wastewater from sinks, toilets, and showers travel through their own separate system of pipes to empty into the city's sewers. The building's drainage pipes measure 30 miles (48 km) long in total. Many have carefully designed bends to slow the wastewater flow, particularly from the highest floors.

Occupying parts of the 40th, 41st, and 42nd floors, a giant reservoir holds even more water than the break tanks.

See also

Find out how water is used in the home (130–131) and how wastewater is collected (132–133).

Powerful pumps in the building's basement move water up to the main reservoir.

Water in space

The International Space Station is an orbital science laboratory with up to six astronauts living in space at a time. It must provide everything humans need to survive—including water. It costs a lot of money to send water into space, so astronauts use it very efficiently, recycling as much as possible. They can even recycle their own urine into drinking water!

The International Space Station has been permanently crewed for 20 years!

Water to be processed

Going to the bathroom is not so simple when floating in space. Astronauts are trained to use a very special toilet designed to keep things clean and capture all liquids.

Liquid waste is collected via a tube with a funnel. Air sucks the liquid away to be processed and recycled.

Solid waste goes into a "commode" and is dried to remove water for recycling.

Tiny droplets of water that astronauts breathe out are also captured and recycled.

The system can even recycle an astronaut's sweat!

No shower in space

There is no shower on the International Space Station—water droplets would float everywhere and cause problems. Instead, astronauts use liquid soap, wet washcloths, and dry shampoo.

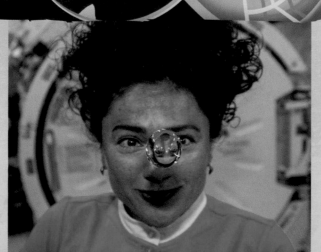

Getting an upgrade

The waste management system is currently being upgraded and will include replacements for the now aging space toilet!

Processing urine

Before it can be treated with the other collected water, urine is treated in the Urine Processor Assembly. This separates the water from the waste.

The urine is distilled—heated up and then cooled to remove salts, which are disposed of.

The water is then cooled in a purge pump and a separator removes unwanted gases.

Water processor assembly

Once the urine has been processed, it can join other collected water waste to be further cleaned, treated, and tested before being supplied back to the astronauts as pure, clean water.

Ready for drinking

Before the astronauts can drink the water, it is tested for quality. If it fails, the water must go through the whole process again.

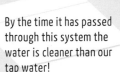

By the time it has passed through this system the water is cleaner than our tap water!

First the water is scanned for small living things called microbes. It is then filtered to remove any leftover particles.

See also
Find out about how water is used to make power (126–127).

The water is passed through filtration beds, which remove any unwanted chemicals. It then goes to the reactor where it is heated and reacted with oxygen to remove organic chemicals.

Pouches and straws

Astronauts use special water pouches, with straws attached, that can be filled from the water processor assembly. If they tried putting water in a glass it would escape.

Glossary

algae simple, plantlike living things that make their own food using energy from sunlight

amphibians group of cold-blooded air-breathing vertebrates with moist skin, usually developing from aquatic larvae (tadpoles); a frog is an amphibian

arteries blood vessels that carry blood that is high in oxygen away from the heart

asexual reproduction a kind of reproduction that does not involve fertilization so that just one parent can produce offspring

atmosphere mass of air that surrounds the Earth

atoms smallest units of matter

aquatic living in or near water

bacteria single-celled microorganisms that can be helpful or harmful

breeding producing offspring (baby organisms) by mating

canyon deep, narrow valley with steep sides

cells living building blocks of organisms

chlorophyll green pigment in plants that helps them absorb the energy of sunlight for photosynthesis

cold-blooded animals that have a body temperature that varies with the environment that they are in

colony number of living things of the same kind that live closely together

condensation change in the state of water from gas to liquid form

continent one of several large landmasses on Earth

courtship animal behavior that forms a bond between a male and a female before mating

crust Earth's hard, outermost layer

density the mass, or amount of material, in a certain volume of space

dialect a variety of language that is found in a particular geographic region

droplet small drop of liquid

echinoderm marine invertebrate, such as a sea urchin or a starfish

eggs fertilized female sex cells that grow into a new animal. Some eggs develop inside the mother's body, others are laid. The eggs of birds and reptiles are enclosed by shells

embryos early stage of development of an animal or plant

endangered at risk of becoming extinct (dying out entirely)

environment area in which a person, plant, or animal lives

erosion way in which sediment formed by weathering gets carried away by wind, running water, or the moving ice of glaciers

evaporation when a liquid changes to a gas

exoskeleton external skeleton that supports and protects an animal's body

extinction when the last individual of a species dies out, so there are no more of its kind alive

fertilization when male and female sex cells unite to form a fertilized egg

freshwater water that is not salty

fetus developing young of an animal before it is born

galaxy very large group of stars and clouds of gas and dust held together by gravity

gills feathery structures on the bodies of animals through which oxygen is absorbed from the water

gravity force that pulls objects together

habitat natural home of an animal or plant

hibernation sleeplike state that helps certain animals survive through winter

hormone a chemical message that is released from a gland into the bloodstream

host living thing that provides food for a parasite

igneous rock rock that forms when magma cools underground or when lava solidifies

invertebrates animals without a backbone

juvenile young animal that is not yet an adult

larva young animal that is quite unlike its parents, and that changes into an adult by complete metamorphosis (plural: larvae)

lava hot, molten rock that erupts onto Earth's surface from volcanoes

litter group of young born to an animal at a single time

magma molten rock flowing under the surface of the Earth

mammal warm-blooded, usually furry animal that feeds its young with milk

mantle thick rocky layer of Earth between the crust and the core

marine linked to or found in the sea or ocean

mating when male and female come together in sexual reproduction so male sperm can fertilize eggs inside the female's body

matriline a social group led by a dominant breeding female; orcas, also called killer whales, live in groups that are matrilines

metamorphic rock rock that forms when existing rocks are changed by heat and pressure to form new rocks

metamorphosis change in body form shown in animals such as insects and amphibians as they grow into adults

microbes tiny living things, such as bacteria

migration the regular, usually yearly, journey made by an animal to and from different places to feed and breed

nutrients substance needed by an organism to live and grow

nymph young insect that looks similar to its parents, but has no wings, and cannot reproduce. Nymphs develop by incomplete metamorphosis

organism living thing

osmosis the way water seeps across a membrane from a low to high concentration of substance

Pangaea supercontinent that existed from about 320–200 million years ago, before breaking up

parasite an organism that lives and feeds on or in another organism, its host, causing the host harm

particle microscopic bit of matter, such as an atom or a molecule

photosynthesis process by which plants and algae make their own food using the energy from sunlight

pods group of sea mammals, such as dolphins or whales

predators animals that hunt other animals for food

pregnant female animal that has a baby growing inside her body

prey animal that is hunted by other animals

pupas resting stage in the life cycle of some insects, during which they develop from larva to adult through a complete change in body shape (metamorphosis)

reptile cold-blooded, scaly-skinned vertebrate, such as a snakes and lizards, that breathe air using lungs

reproduction production of offspring (young)

saltwater water found in seas and oceans

schools large number of fish or other aquatic animals swimming together

sediment tiny pieces of rock, the remains of living things, or chemical deposits that settle on the beds of lakes, rivers, and oceans

sedimentary rock rock made from sediment. Layers of sediment get squashed and cemented together until they form rock

seeds capsules containing a plant embryo and its food supply

sex cell cell that is either male (sperm cell) or female (egg cell) involved in reproduction

sexual reproduction reproduction involving fertilization of egg by sperm

sperm male sex cell

spores single cell that is produced by a fungus or plant, and can grow into a new individual

tadpoles larva of a frog or toad. Tadpoles breathe through gills rather than lungs, and they have a long tail

tectonic plate one of the pieces that make up Earth's rigid shell

territory area claimed by an animal, which it defends against rivals

transpiration loss of water by evaporation from plant leaves

uterus also called a womb, part of a female mammal's body in which a baby develops before it is born

vapor water that exists in its gaseous state

veins blood vessels that carry blood that is low in oxygen back to the heart

vertebrates animals with a backbone

weathering when rocks and minerals are worn down into sediment

Index

Acknowledgments

The publisher would like to thank the following for their kind permission to reproduce their photographs:

(Key: a-above; b-below/bottom; c-center; f-far; l-left; r-right; t-top)

6 Dreamstime.com: Paop (bl). 6-7 123RF.com: Polsin Junpangpen. 7 Alamy Stock Photo: ACORN 1 (ca); Nature Picture Library / SCOTLAND: The Big Picture (bl). Dreamstime.com: Flatbox2 (cl); Okea (br). naturepl.com: Jussi Murtosaari (tc). 8-9 123RF.com: Polsin Junpangpen. 9 NASA: Goddard Space Flight Center Scientific Visualization Studio (cra). 10-11 123RF.com: Polsin Junpangpen. 14-15 123RF.com: Polsin Junpangpen. 14 123RF.com: nasaimages (tr). Dreamstime.com: Leonidtit (cl); Mike Ricci (crb); Phanuwatn (br). Getty Images / iStock: PongMoji (clb). 15 123RF.com: Anna Yakimova (cb). Alamy Stock Photo: Frans Lemmens (cla). Dreamstime.com: Bidouze St¥Ë_phane (crb). Getty Images / iStock: Ray Hems (tr); phototropic (bc). 16 Getty Images / iStock: Photon-Photos (cb). 17 Alamy Stock Photo: Stocktrek Images, Inc. / Walter Myers (cb). 18 Getty Images / iStock: mdesigner125 (bc). 19 Dreamstime.com: Gino Rigucci (bl). Shutterstock.com: Pike-28 (br). 20 Dreamstime.com: Parin Parmar (cra). 21 Dreamstime.com: Jarosław Janczuk (tc); Lesley Mcewan (clb); New Person (cra). 23 Alamy Stock Photo: Paul Wood (br). Getty Images: Jose Jimenez (cra). NOAA: (crb). 25 123RF.com: Andrew Mayovskyy / jojjik (cra). Getty Images: E+ / ra-photos (br). © Jenny E. Ross: (crb). 27 Dreamstime.com: Tomas Griger (br). Getty Images: Michele Falzone (crb). naturepl.com: Doug Allan (cra). 29 Depositphotos Inc: MyGoodImages (tr). Shutterstock.com: Eva Mont (crb). 30 Depositphotos Inc: ilfede (bc). 30-31 Alamy Stock Photo: Gerner Thomsen (bc). 31 Dreamstime.com: Igor Groshev / Igorspb (bc). 33 Alamy Stock Photo: Jerónimo Alba (crb); Peter Adams Photography (cra); Nature Picture Library / Anup Shah (br). 35 Alamy Stock Photo: Rupesh Sethi (crb); Tom Till (cra). Dreamstime.com: Jon Helgason (br). 36 NASA: Jacques Descloitres, MODIS Rapid Response Team / GSFC (bl). 36-37 Shutterstock.com: Deni_Sugandi (bc). 37 Alamy Stock Photo: ARCTIC IMAGES / Ragnar Th Sigurdsson (bc). 39 Dreamstime.com: Javarman (tr). NASA: Goddard Space Flight Center Scientific Visualization Studio (crb). 40 Getty Images / iStock: abriendomundo (bl). 41 Alamy Stock Photo: Robertharding / Christian Kober (br). Fotolia: Yong Hian Lim (bl). 42 Dreamstime.com: Raldi Somers / Raldi (bl). 42-43 Dreamstime.com: Martin Schneiter (bc). 43 123RF.com: Yongyut Kumsri (bc). 44 Getty Images / iStock: andrej67 (br). 45 Getty Images / iStock: RyuSeungil (bl). 46 Shutterstock.com: EPA-EFE / Darren Pateman (cl). 47 Alamy Stock Photo: Husky29 (bl); mauritius images GmbH / Reinhard Dirscherl (cr). 51 NOAA: Mountains in the Sea Research Team; the IFE Crew; and NOAA / OAR / OER. (crb); Pacific Ring of Fire 2004 Expedition. NOAA Office of Ocean Exploration; Dr. Bob Embley, NOAA PMEL, Chief Scientist. (tr). 54 Alamy Stock Photo: Nigel Cattlin (bl). Getty Images / iStock: alexei_tm (cla). 54-55 123RF.com: Polsin Junpangpen. 55 Alamy Stock Photo: Nigel Cattlin (crb). Getty Images / iStock: alexei_tm (br). 57 Alamy Stock Photo: mediasculp (tr). Getty Images / iStock: E+ / apomares (br). 58 Robert Harding Picture Library: Okapia / Hermann Eisenbeiss (ca). 59 Alamy Stock Photo: Avalon. red / Oceans Image (crb); imageBROKER / Siegfried Grassegger (tr); PF-(usna1) (ca). naturepl.com: Pete Oxford (bc). SuperStock: Minden Pictures (clb). 60 Getty Images / iStock: E+ / chee gin tan (bc). 60-61 Getty Images / iStock: Rodrusoleg (br). 61 Shutterstock.com: Maximumm (br). 63 Dreamstime.com: Liliia Khuzhakhmetova (br). naturepl.com: Simon Colmer (tr); David Shale (cr). 64 Alamy Stock Photo: Andrew DuBois (crb). naturepl.

com: Michael & Patricia Fogden (cla). SuperStock: Minden Pictures / Buiten-beeld / Chris Stenger (tr). 65 Dreamstime.com: Igor Kovalchuk (ca). naturepl.com: Melvin Grey (cra). 66 Dreamstime.com: Björn Wylezich (bc). 66-67 123RF.com: Balash Mirzabey (bc). 67 Dreamstime.com: Valmedia Creatives (br). 70-71 123RF.com: Polsin Junpangpen. 70 123RF.com: Marc Henauer (tr). Alamy Stock Photo: Wildestanimal (cl). Dreamstime.com: Aquanaut4 (clb). Getty Images: Roland Birke (crb). naturepl.com: Fred Bavendam (br). 71 Alamy Stock Photo: Andrey Nekrasov (br); WaterFrame_fba (cla). Dreamstime.com: Steven Melanson / Xscream1 (tr). naturepl.com: Doug Allan (crb). Shutterstock.com: Arm001 (cb). 72 Alamy Stock Photo: BIOSPHOTO / Sergio Hanquet (cb); Paulo Oliveira (cl). Dreamstime.com: Vitalyedush (cb). 73 naturepl.com: Solvin Zankl (clb). 74 Alamy Stock Photo: Allstar Picture Library Ltd. (cl). 75 Alamy Stock Photo: Nature Photographers Ltd / Paul R. Sterry (cl); Martin Shields (cra). Dreamstime.com: Photographyfirm (ca). 76 Alamy Stock Photo: Sabena Jane Blackbird (c). Dreamstime.com: Tjkphotography (cla). 77 Alamy Stock Photo: John Henderson (crb); R Kawka (cb). Getty Images: Cavan Images (bl). naturepl.com: Mark Carwardine (c). 79 Alamy Stock Photo: Images & Stories (br); Stephen Frink Collection (tr); Visual&Written SL / KELVIN AITKEN / VWPICS (crb). 81 Alamy Stock Photo: Nature Picture Library / Franco Banfi (br); Paulo Oliveira (cra). 82 Alamy Stock Photo: Buiten-Beeld / Nico van Kappel (bc). 82-83 Alamy Stock Photo: FLPA (bc). 83 Getty Images / iStock: AlbyDeTweede (br). naturepl.com: Robert Thompson (bc). 84 Alamy Stock Photo: blickwinkel / Hartl (clb). Dreamstime.com: Mirkorosenau (cla). Science Photo Library: Eye Of Science (bl). 87 Alamy Stock Photo: Minden Pictures (crb); Andrey Nekrasov (br). naturepl.com: Gary Bell / Oceanwide (cra). 89 Alamy Stock Photo: Bazzano Photography (br); blickwinkel / F. Teigler (crb). naturepl.com: Eduardo Blanco (cra). 91 Alamy Stock Photo: Agefotostock / Georgie Holland (crb); Andrey Nekrasov (cra). Dreamstime.com: Selahattin Ünsal Karhan / Porbeagle (br). 92 Alamy Stock Photo: imageBROKER / Norbert Probst (bl). 92-93 Alamy Stock Photo: Michael Patrick O'Neill (bc). 93 Alamy Stock Photo: WaterFrame_fur (br). 94 Dreamstime.com: Marc Henauer (br). Getty Images / iStock: E+ / SeppFriedhuber (bl). 95 Getty Images / iStock: Frankhildebrand (br). 97 Dreamstime.com: Michael Valos (br). Getty Images: Sjoerd Bosch (cr). naturepl.com: Todd Pusser (cra). 98 Alamy Stock Photo: Mike Read (bl). 98-99 Alamy Stock Photo: FLPA / Richard Costin (bc). 99 Dreamstime.com: David Herraez (br). 100 Dreamstime.com: Ben Mcleish / Benmm (bl). 101 Dreamstime.com: Oreena (bl). naturepl.com: Jurgen Freund (br). 102 Alamy Stock Photo: Nature Picture Library / Claudio Contreras (br); Scenics & Science (bl). 103 Alamy Stock Photo: Nature Picture Library (br). 104 Alamy Stock Photo: Nature Picture Library (bl). Shutterstock.com: SergeUWPhoto (br). 105 Dreamstime.com: Shakeelmsm (bl). 106 Alamy Stock Photo: Reinhard Dirscherl (bl); Fabrice Bettex Photography (br). 107 Alamy Stock Photo: Helmut Corneli (br); National Geographic Image Collection (bc). 108 Alamy Stock Photo: Nature Picture Library / Solvin Zankl (tl). SuperStock: Steve Downeranth / Pantheon (tc). 109 Alamy Stock Photo: Nature Picture Library / Doug Perrine (br). Science Photo Library: Sonke Johnsen / Visuals Unlimited, Inc. (tl). 111 Dorling Kindersley: Hunterian Museum University of Glasgow (tr). Getty Images / iStock: borchee (br). 112 naturepl.com: Mike Parry (bc). 113 Alamy Stock Photo: Nature Picture Library / Pete Oxford (br); RGB Ventures / SuperStock / Scubazoo (bl). 115 Alamy Stock Photo: blickwinkel / McPHOTO / RMU (br); Adrian Hepworth (cra); SBS Eclectic Images (bl). 116 naturepl.com: Piotr Naskrecki (bc); Visuals Unlimited (bl). 117 Dreamstime.com: Isselee (br). 119 Dreamstime.com: Melvinlee (tr). Getty Images / iStock: vojce (cr). naturepl.com: Kevin Schafer (br). 121

Alamy Stock Photo: Premaphotos (tr); Scenics & Science (cra). Getty Images: Moment / Douglas Klug (br). 124-125 123RF.com: Polsin Junpangpen. 124 123RF.com: Phuong Nguyen Duy (tr). Dreamstime.com: Jaoueichi (br). Getty Images / iStock: danefromspain (cl). 125 Dreamstime.com: Lightfieldstudiosprod (tc). Getty Images / iStock: chuyu (b); MAGNIFIER (ca). 126 Alamy Stock Photo: Les. Ladbury (tr). 127 Alamy Stock Photo: Global Warming Images / Ashley Cooper (cla). Getty Images: The Image Bank / Kim Steele (cra). Getty Images / iStock: Reimphoto (tc). 128 Dreamstime.com: Heritage Pictures (tr); Nd3000 (cr). 129 Dreamstime.com: Suwin Puengsamrong (tc). Shutterstock.com: Kent Raney (cr). 131 123RF.com: Chayatorn Laorattanavech (cra). Dreamstime.com: Nikkytok (crb); Igor Yegorov (br). 132 Dreamstime.com: Ludmila Smite (bl). 133 Getty Images / iStock: Picsfive (br). 134 Getty Images / iStock: pidjoe (br). 135 Alamy Stock Photo: Picture Partners (bc). 136 Alamy Stock Photo: Geopix (bc); NG Images (br).
137 NASA: JSC PAO Web Team / Amiko Kauderer (bc)

All other images © Dorling Kindersley
For further information see: www.dkimages.com

DK would like to thank:
Helen Peters for compiling the index and Caroline Stamps for proofreading.

About the illustrator
Sam Falconer is an illustrator with a particular interest in science and nature. He has illustrated content for publications including *National Geographic, Scientific American,* and *New Scientist*. This is his second children's book.